T0157637

DELIVERING WOMEN FROM THE SNARES OF DEATH

PURGING SIN TO PROSPER THE SOUL

PAIGE COLEMAN

WESTBOW
PRESS
A DIVISION OF THOMAS NELSON

WestBow Press books may be ordered through booksellers or by contacting:

WestBow Press
A Division of Thomas Nelson
1663 Liberty Drive
Bloomington, IN 47403
www.westbowpress.com
1-(866) 928-1240

ISBN: 978-1-4908-0582-5 (sc)
ISBN: 978-1-4908-0584-9 (hc)
ISBN: 978-1-4908-0583-2 (e)

Library of Congress Control Number: 2013915117

Printed in the United States of America.

WestBow Press rev. date: 08/26/2013

The pangs of death compassed me, and the torrents of ungodliness troubled me exceedingly. The pangs of hell came round about me: the snares of death prevented me.
(Psalm 18:4-5 LXX)

DEDICATION

With humility and joy, I daily acknowledge the presence of the Lord Jesus Christ in my heart and dedicate this labour of love to Him, for His glory.

Secondly, to my husband whose strength, integrity, and self-sacrifice have in our marriage been a faithful representation of the relationship between Christ and His church. Thank you for making it easy to love, honour, and obey you.

FOREWORD

By Peter Coleman

As I begin this foreword I must first give recognition to the One that made it all possible, Jesus Christ the Lamb of God, a person of the trinity. The Father's love sent Him to atone for our sins. His sinless life and obedience to the Father's will established His righteousness. By dying on a cross meant for criminals, He shed His blood to atone for the sins of the world. His subsequent resurrection from death made it possible for my sins to be forgiven and my eyes to be opened. I am saved, not by my power, but by His holy and selfless sacrifice; He exchanged my sins for His righteousness. To you, Lord, be all the glory, honour, and praise now and for ever. Amen.

Who is Paige Coleman and how can she speak as an authority on this matter? Sure, she has spent many years in university—even secured for herself a Master's degree with distinction in Anthropology. It's all rubbish in my opinion, especially when none of it was saving her soul from hell. Like Solomon said, **all is vanity** (Ecclesiastes 1:2b LXX). She grew up in a pseudo-Christian environment that did little to establish the credibility and reality of the All-Mighty. In conjunction, public school and post-secondary institutions of "higher learning", and other worldly influences did a splendid job in her younger years to lead her, step-by-step, toward the gates of hell.

When we met I realized right away that she was a boat being tossed in the ocean, trying to convince herself that her life was normal. I began to share the gospel with her and answer every question or debating point she had about God. Simply put, I was ready to **answer words of truth to them that question thee** (Proverbs 22:21b LXX). This was not because I was the apostle Paul reborn, but because when I was freed myself by Christ,

I was determined never to be deceived again. I had spent un-tolled hours researching the Bible, world history, and the sciences. I was saved through faith in Him, but now knew the proof of Him.

Praise be to God in the highest, Paige heard the voice of the Shepherd, and was saved. Since then she has dedicated her life to Him in every way. She has since had some royal battles with her flesh, resisting the sin within her, determined to do the Master's will. She realized, as I had explained to her early on, that to deny certain things about God as outlined in scripture while accepting others is to deny the God-inspired nature of scripture. The person that does this is committing idolatry. Understanding this, she read and memorized the Word daily, striving to walk closer to the God of the Bible.

Like an amazing metamorphosis from caterpillar to butterfly, my wife has transformed from a struggling new Christian to a God-blessed Titus 2 woman. She is my glory, and another proof that God's Word is truth and profitable for instruction. She feels the peace and joy that come from knowing God's will. How does she know God's will? She reads the Bible. It really is as simple as that.

Paige is spoken of by fellow Christians as a tremendous example of a Biblical woman, wife, and mother. My unchristian colleagues think that she is incredible and wish they were married to one such as her. This reinforces what I already know about my wife. She is not perfect, but she sure is getting there. At this point, I believe she will heap more treasure at the feet of our Lord than I will. God bless you, honey.

Ultimately, this is a book written by a Christian woman for Christian women. This does not mean that men cannot profit from reading it; in fact, they would profit greatly. I also think it is important for—and the responsibility of—a husband or father to discern the Biblical accuracy of Christian literature. Remember that **a little leaven leaveneth the whole lump** (1 Corinthians 5:6). A little bit of poison makes the whole meal poisonous. Therefore, it is critical that we do not arbitrarily call something Christian because someone else calls it so, but only after testing it against the scriptures. I have every confidence that if tested faithfully against the Word, this book will stand.

Enjoy, be edified, seek His face, and be blessed.

Peter

PREFACE

S everal years ago it occurred to me that for me to be a Christian, I needed to know Christ well enough to do what He required of me. King David said to God, **I have hidden thine oracles**[1] **in my heart, that I might not sin against thee** (Psalm 119:11 LXX). David knew that the best way to keep from sinning against God was to learn His Word and do what it says. From that day forward I strove to follow his example. I did more than just read the Word each day—I began to memorize it so that His commandments would abide in my heart. The outcome was astonishing. A process of change was begun in me to bring the way I thought, spoke, and behaved under obedience to Christ.

Almost immediately I discovered that the blessings from above began to pour out on me. I experienced peace of mind, solace, joy, and wisdom. My mind was renewed. I was inspired and hopeful. The things of this world began to dull, darken, and disappear. I was walking closer to Christ and I was living in His will. None of this resulted from my own merit, but from the righteousness of Jesus Christ, whose grace is sufficient for all of us.

A few years later while perusing an online Q&A for Christian women, I noticed that almost every question women asked had an answer in God's Word. I was inspired to use scripture to supply some of those answers. After two years of writing, I was able to draw two profound but troubling conclusions. The first was that **all seek their own, not the things which are Jesus Christ's** (Philippians 2:21) and the second was that there is a great need for Christian women to mentor others based not on their

---

[1] King David uses the word "oracle" the same way he uses the word "commandment", "law", "prophecy", or "Word" of God. In other words, King David wants to keep all of God's words in his heart to both remember and do them.

own "wisdom", but on the **wisdom that descendeth from above** (James 3:17a).

Soon I was inspired to address these problems by writing a book for women. My intention was threefold. First, I was so full of enthusiasm and joy over how God's Word had blessed me that I wanted to share that joy with my fellow sisters in Christ. Second, I wanted to encourage women to seek God's will, not their own, so that their joy could be full. And third, it is my heart's desire to elevate the Word of God to its rightful position as the ultimate authority over us all. If it were recognized as such, all counsel would be sought from it, not from the world, and not from the grossly exaggerated estimation of human authority.

As I sat down to write, I rejoiced at being counted worthy to labour in Jesus' Name for the benefit of other women like me who love the Lord, who want to learn about Him, grow closer to Him, and be blessed. I realized that many women do not have the benefit of sound Bible teaching. They have many questions that too few are able to answer justly, truthfully, or righteously. It became both a joy and an obligation to impart many of the lessons the good Lord had taught me to others, and it is my most sincere desire to see others benefit from the same.

There are two things that I can say with relative certainty about this book. First, it has the potential to deeply offend you (I apologize in advance!). Second, it will be very much worth it in the end (I rejoice with you in advance!). God bless you as you take on this challenge, for Him and for His glory wrought courageously through you.

It is my privilege to acknowledge my dearest sister for ironing out the early wrinkles, my father for poring over the scriptural details, and my gracious Titus 2 mother for penning the Bible study. I must also thank my intrepid editor for his diligence and encouragement, and a special thanks to a new and dear friend, A.T. Most importantly, my heart rejoices in the love and encouragement freely given me by my husband whose Biblical insight, spiritual discernment, and boldness in Christ have never ceased to incur my respect and admiration.

Thank you.

Paige

CONTENTS

INTRODUCTION

I was never a perfect woman, nor do I claim to have been. In fact, I can assure you that I have made every mistake in this book! I am neither glorious nor worthy of your admiration; but I know the One who is. He is the Lord Jesus Christ, Son of the living God, the Lord of glory. He has given us the truth in His written Word for us to profit by. **All scripture is given by inspiration of God, and is profitable for doctrine, for reproof, for correction, for instruction in righteousness: That the man of God may be perfect, thoroughly furnished unto all good works** (2 Timothy 3:16-17).

It is for this reason that I fully intend, without apology, to quote the words of our precious Lord and Saviour as often as possible. There is no understanding, authority, or truth apart from the Word of God.

I have read "Christian" books whose authors either quote, misquote, or paraphrase God's Word as a single verse at the beginning of a chapter. They proceed to pen pages and pages of personal opinions that have departed from the Biblical truth. The more they rely on their self-appointed authority, the more their words become inundated with unsubstantiated humanist claims that openly contradict the Bible. They stray so far from reality that they become guilty of spreading false doctrine. These authors are dangerous and are to be avoided. They have assisted in the devil's efforts to lead us astray. I have no intention of incurring God's wrath by following suit. It is for this reason that I ask you to check what I have written against the Word of God. If I am in error, do not choose to believe me. Choose to believe the Bible.

What tends to happen when reading the Holy Scriptures is a tug at the conscience—to put it mildly. For some, reading the Word of God is far more than a tug; it is more like a violent wrenching! It can be downright uncomfortable. The Bible verses coupled with the information in this book may have a similar effect. Please do not cower in anticipation of it. It is the chastening of the Lord (1 Corinthians 11:32), which He reserves for His beloved children (Hebrews 12:7). Although it may at first be grievous, **nevertheless afterward it yieldeth the peaceable fruit of righteousness unto them which are exercised thereby** (Hebrews 12:11). When you feel the nudge or the pull, or the pounding, or the yanking, or the still, small voice—stop. Stop and offer your Father in heaven your most sincere gratitude. He chastens those He loves.

Chastening is to be both expected and embraced if we are to learn from our Father in heaven who loves us enough to admonish us. I ask you, therefore, to be not dismayed if you are so convicted, but rejoice. I can assure you that the everlasting reward will be worth the temporary discomfort.

The Word of God **is a discerner of the thoughts and intents of the heart** (Hebrews 4:12b). It is an incredible and edifying experience to recognize the darkness of your own heart. Incredible because you could not have predicted what you saw, and edifying because you could not have worked harder to make it go. Because the Word laid my heart bare, exposing the dirt within, I was able—and continue to strive—to systematically deal with the character flaws that manifest themselves in my life. This book is designed to lay these flaws bare for you, so that you can learn to recognize them and overcome them with the Lord's help. Since it is God **which searcheth the reins and hearts** (Revelation 2:23b), I ask that you read with this attitude: **Prove me, O God, and know my heart; examine me, and know my paths; and see if there is any way of iniquity in me, and lead me in an everlasting way** (Psalm 139:23-24 LXX).

For the glory of the Lord, I changed for the better. You can change, too. If you have willing hands and a contrite heart, the Lord will bring you closer to Him and you will abide in His will. His blessings will abound, and you will rejoice in your deliverance.

The main part of this book will be a compilation of examples provided for us by the Bible. Because it is written by a woman, for women, I will focus on female examples. When I began my search through scripture, I was surprised to find so many gloomy stories pertaining specifically to women. Each snapshot triggered a warning bell for me. I was either convicted in a current area of my life or taught a lesson in advance. I am still learning. Because my desire to live for the Lord outweighed my desire to live for myself, I was delighted to learn how to avoid incurring His displeasure. I hope you will too.

My initial example search gave me a nineteen-point list. I have condensed it to six, the number of sin, and qualified them with both modern and Biblical adjectives. See if any of these descriptors resonate in your heart:

1. Foolish (self-deceived, self-destructive)
2. Stubborn (hard-hearted, disobedient)
3. Clamorous (contentious, striving)
4. Wanton (unfulfilled, shameless)
5. Idle (lazy, unfruitful)
6. Usurping (avaricious, rebellious)

As you read through this list, did you think of any way these adjectives apply to you? Each word will be described thoroughly for you in context in the upcoming chapters. I will give you a Biblical example as well as a modern example of each profile so that you can learn to identify and avoid cultivating these traits in yourself and over-exposing yourself to these traits in others. Please apply each word to yourself first and not to another woman you know. This book is not intended to give you ammunition against the women in your life. It is intended to help you improve your own life.

These six traits are examples of the **works of the flesh** (Galatians 5:19a). Not one of them, if left unchecked, leads to eternal life (Galatians 5:21b). They are examples of the snares of corruption and ungodliness which lead to eternal death. They can and must be *purged*, so that you can become a **vessel unto honour, sanctified, and meet for the master's use, and prepared unto every good work** (2 Timothy 2:21b).

The Biblical examples are applicable to both men and women and are illustrated Biblically by both men and women. However, I have designed them to help women. Therefore, throughout this book, I address women but retain the old English use of the term "man" when quoting scripture. The King James English uses the term "man" generically unless context dictates otherwise. Please apply this term to yourself as you read. For example, the following verse applies to you: **For by the hearing of these a wise man will be wiser, and a man of understanding will gain direction** (Proverbs 1:5 LXX).

There will be a positive example in the seventh chapter of this book for you to look forward to: 7. Blessed (prospered, fulfilled). Please persevere and read to the end!

At the end of each chapter is a section entitled "Think on These Things", considerately submitted by my 67-year-old mother. It is based on Philippians 4:8-9:

> **Finally, brethren, whatsoever things are true, whatsoever things are honest, whatsoever things are just, whatsoever things are pure, whatsoever things are lovely, whatsoever things are of good report, if there be any virtue, and if there be any praise, think on these things. Those things, which ye have both learned, and received, and heard, and seen in me, do: and the God of peace shall be with you.**

Bible verses have been included as a help for reassurance and study.

Thy law is a lamp to my feet, and a light to my paths (Psalm 119:105 LXX). I pray that this book will bear sufficient truth, that the references to the Word of God may outnumber all others, and that no single reader will choose to accept my words without first accepting the wisdom that is from above, which is **first pure, then peaceable, gentle, and easy to be intreated, full of mercy and good fruits, without partiality, and without hypocrisy** (James 3:17).

A Note on Bible Versions

The Bible verses quoted from the New Testament are from *The Holy Bible*, Authorized King James Version. For information about understanding this version's vocabulary and grammar, I recommend that you watch Gail Riplinger's "English Lesson" on youtube.

For the Old Testament, I quote Sir Lancelot C.L. Brenton's *Septuagint with Apocrypha: Greek and English* (1851). I do this for a few reasons. First, the Greek Old Testament words spoken by Jesus and the apostles in the New Testament are directly quoted from the Greek Septuagint. No other Old Testament contains these quotations word for word as Jesus spoke them. Second, the Septuagint contains every prophecy fulfilled in the New Testament while some are missing from other Old Testament Bible versions. Third, Brenton's English translation corresponds beautifully with the New Testament KJV, making cross referencing and word comparisons easy as well as profitable. Its usage will be indicated by the Roman numeral for 70, which is "LXX", following the verse reference.

In a few instances, I have referred to *The Book of Jasher*.[1] This is meant to elucidate the Biblical account. It is not intended to reflect the opinion that *The Book of Jasher* is inspired. This book, although referred to in scripture,[2] is not included in the Biblical canon.

For purposes of clarity, I use common names for all Old Testament characters instead of the names rendered from the Greek in the Septuagint. For example, Eli and his sons, Hophni and Phinheas, will be written as such. In the Septuagint, the names would have been Heli, Ophni and Phinees. I would rather not cause the reader any unnecessary furrowing of the eye brows over such a simple matter. Similarly, I will use common book titles. For example, in the Septuagint, I & II Samuel are I & II Kings, and I & II Kings are called III and IV Kings. I make these alterations for the reader's ease as well as my own and intend no malfeasance toward either Biblical source.

> **If any man speak, let him speak as the oracles of God;**
> **if any man minister, let him do it as of the ability which**
> **God giveth: that God in all things may be glorified**
> **through Jesus Christ, to whom be praise and dominion**
> **for ever and ever. Amen.**
> (1 Peter 4:11)

---

[1] *The Book of Jasher* (Springville, UT: Cedar Fort, 2010).

[2] See Joshua 10:13 and 2 Samuel 1:18.

CHAPTER ONE

KNOW WISDOM AND INSTRUCTION

PROVERBS 1:2 LXX

The Bible contains instruction for virtually every facet of human life. Many of the examples are negatives, for us to learn by. In other words, the Bible teaches us what not to do. It gives us examples of disobedient people who suffer the consequences of their sin. The hapless Israelites, God's chosen people, provide many such examples. Will you learn from them?

In reference to their disobedience in the wilderness under Moses, Paul tells us, **Now all these things happened unto them for ensamples: and they are written for our admonition, upon whom the ends of the world are come. Wherefore let him that thinketh he standeth take heed lest he fall** (1 Corinthians 10:11-12). Some of us have clear outward vision but are blind when we look inward. We so readily see the fault that is our sister's but so rarely see the fault that is our own. **And why beholdest thou the mote that is in thy brother's eye, but perceivest not the beam that is in thine own eye?** (Luke 6:41). It is often when we think we stand the tallest that we are in for a fall. If you look into your heart with a sincere desire to see the truth, humility will lay bare your needs, and you will not be deceived. **Humble yourself in the sight of the Lord, and he shall lift you up** (James 4:10).

In many cases, I did not recognize that I manifested the works of the flesh (Galatians 5:19a) until they were revealed to me by scripture. **For the**

Word of God is quick, and powerful, and sharper than any twoedged sword, piercing even to the dividing asunder of soul and spirit, and of the joints and marrow (Hebrews 4:12a). Do you seek this kind of clarity? Are you willing to open your heart and let the light in? If you acknowledge problem areas in your life with honesty and integrity, with a sincere desire to change them for your eternal reward and for God's unforeseeable glory, then you will be blessed. **The night is far spent, the day is at hand: let us therefore cast off the works of darkness, and let us put on the armour of light** (Romans 13:12).

Walking in the Flesh

I was saved from eternal death and hell when I was thirty years old. Peter Coleman shared the gospel with me, convinced me of my sin, and led me to Christ. Did I immediately stop sinning the very next day? No. I was still a creature of habit, and had formed behavioural tendencies that took a long time and God's grace to break free from. Although I don't blame anyone but myself for keeping those bad habits for as long as I did, I must identify one of the biggest obstacles to my change: the mediocrity of the "church". Let me explain.

Attending typical churches in my area did little to improve my relationship with Christ. Many of the Christian women around me were no different from their worldly, lost counterparts. Like women of the world, they gathered together to talk about everything *but* God. Why weren't these believing, Christian women gathering together to edify and encourage one another in Christ? Did they not feel indebted to the Lord and relieved to know that they, too, were saved from eternal death and hell? Why were they not acting like it, and why were they not studying their Bibles and living a Biblical life?

To my dismay, I found that many of these women ruled the home, leaving their husbands neglected and disparaged. Others clearly wanted to rule the church, striving for status that would give them earthly recognition. They were loud sometimes in voice and outspoken, conducting themselves more like men than like women. I even found some who tried to cajole me into behaving more like the world! Some didn't talk about what they *could* accomplish in Christ, but about what they *couldn't* accomplish. The only part Christ played in the latter conversation was that He was blamed for not doing things differently.

The state I found myself in could be explained in many ways (a church body unaware of the satanic devices within their midst, a congregation brainwashed by evolutionist propaganda, a culture of compromised Christianity, a lack of faith in scriptural authority), but you can explore those reasons for yourself (and I encourage you to do so).[1] The bottom line is that for me, in the early stages of my Christian walk, when I was but a baby, "church" women let me down. Not one of them had what my soul yearned for. The very women from whom I sought godly direction and instruction led me instead toward a numb spiritual life characterized not by the victory we have in Christ, but by the loss we have in this world.

Simply put, our flesh strives to attain the things of this world but our spirit desires the nourishment of the Word. The two are oppositional. They are at enmity one with the other (Galatians 5:17). The saved in Christ yearn for spiritual fulfillment that the world cannot provide. One cannot strive to enter in at the straight gate (Luke 13:24) with cumbersome flesh effectively pulling her back.

That "cumbersome flesh" is found not only in ourselves, but also among the women we know who do little to validate, confirm, defend, or build up our faith. If we find mediocrity in the church, I daresay that we are not in the church (as God defines it). Where are we? We are in the world, and the world is no place for the church. We belong to Christ and our home is in heaven.

What do you see in the women around you? Are they happy? Do they smile sweetly at their husbands, at their children? Do their words resound with scriptural references and a clear knowledge of God? Do they enjoy serving the members of their *own* households? Have they shared their salvation story with you? What themes characterize their speech?

As you ponder the answers to these questions, does your heart grieve for your sisters in Christ? Do you despair over the thoughts of your own

---

[1]   For more on these subjects, read Ken Ham, *The Lie:Evolution/Millions of Years* (Green Forest, AR: Master Books, 1987) or Steve Ham *In God We Trust: Why Biblical Authority Matters for Every Believer* (Green Forest, AR: Master Books, 2010).

heart? I see women who fall so short of their potential in Christ that I despair for their very souls. This grief led me to question the validity of Scripture. I began to search through the Bible, attempting to locate reasons for this overwhelming discrepancy among women who claimed to be Christian, but didn't follow Christ. What I found is the content of this book. It is the answer to these plaguing questions that the child of God asks when she wonders how to serve Christ faithfully in a world that is characterized by compromise and hypocrisy.

Walking in the Spirit

Most of us think that perfection is impossible, so we don't even try to be perfect. If we were perfect, we wouldn't need a Saviour, right? But I want you to understand what the Bible teaches about this. God tells us that it is the Saviour who makes us perfect (Colossians 1:22). Jesus Christ washes our sins away (Psalm 51:7 LXX). He clothes us in righteousness (Ephesians 4:24). He fills us with His Holy Spirit (1 Corinthians 6:19). In Him, we are reborn (1 Peter 1:23). In Him, we are a new person (2 Corinthians 5:17). In Him, we are redeemed (Revelation 5:9). In Him, we are completely secure (John 10:28).

Yes, we still sin. For as long as we are in the flesh, we are prone to sin. Paul addresses this dilemma: **This I say then, Walk in the Spirit, and ye shall not fulfil the lust of the flesh** (Galatians 5:16). For as long as we are walking in the Spirit, we are blameless, righteous, and perfect. This is why the Lord encourages us to make perfection our goal. He says, **Be ye therefore perfect, even as your Father in heaven is perfect** (Matthew 5:48). It is not the Spirit that causes us to fall or to sin; it is the flesh. It is for this reason that Paul writes, **And they that are Christ's have crucified the flesh with the affections and lusts** (Galatians 5:24).

Paul encouraged Timothy to be a good example of the **believers, in word, in conversation, in charity, in spirit, in faith, in purity** (1 Timothy 4:12b). Paul himself was an example of **how holily and justly and unblameably we behaved ourselves among you that believe** (1 Thessalonians 2:10b). These men of God walked in the Spirit of the Lord (while alive on this earth!). Such living is no less attainable for you than it was for them.

Paul, a man who acknowledged himself to be chief among sinners (1 Timothy 1:15), calling his own flesh wretched (Romans 7:24), yet knew that he served God wholly in Spirit (Romans 1:9). I want to assure you that if you believe on the Lord Jesus Christ, having worked out your salvation with fear and trembling (Philippians 2:12), you have the ability to serve God *perfectly* in the Spirit, too. God is able to **Make you perfect in every good work to do his will, working in you that which is wellpleasing in his sight, through Jesus Christ** (Hebrews 13:21a).

If you were to run a race, would you run aimlessly? Would you be content just to start, or would you train yourself to finish? Paul said, **I press toward the mark for the prize of the high calling of God in Christ Jesus. Let us therefore, as many as be perfect, be thus minded** (Philippians 3:14-15a). Only by training our bodies in the ways of a champion could we ever hope to be a champion. So it is with spiritual training. We must take on the necessary self-discipline in order to run the race and cross the finish line. It can be done. Before he died, Paul said, **I have fought a good fight, I have finished my course, I have kept the faith** (2 Timothy 4:7).

The Lord told us to be perfect for a reason. It was to make us fellow labourers with Christ as children of the living God. Through Him—through His Spirit, His Word, and His strength—we can accomplish the impossible. God has given us His Word for that very purpose: so that **the man of God may be perfect, thoroughly furnished unto all good works** (2 Timothy 3:17).

Perfection *is* possible when we aim high and determine to keep our eyes fixed on Christ. Like Paul, we can serve perfectly in Spirit, because the Spirit that is in believers is Holy (1 Corinthians 3:17). Our hope is also assured in that ultimately, our race will be over when our regenerated bodies will be like Christ's—perfect, sinless, and eternal.

God did not promise that the crucifixion of the flesh would be pleasant. It certainly wasn't pleasant for me! And yet, it was—and remains to be—absolutely essential to my growth (and to your growth) in Christ. Without having undertaken the pains of truly surrendering my will and my "Self"[2] to God, there could have been no deliverance from the sin that had beset me. So it must be with all of those who name the name of Jesus Christ as their Lord and Saviour with sincerity.

Spiritual Growing Pains

Now all these things happened unto them for ensamples: and they are written for our admonition (1 Corinthians 10:11). Admonition is "gentle rebuke".[3] God wants us to learn how to please Him so that He can bless us. The Word is our textbook, the Holy Spirit is our teacher, and God is our examiner. We must be diligent students and learn from all three if we are to walk in the Spirit.

Too often we resist His chastisement in preference for our own way. **All we as sheep have gone astray; every one has gone astray in his way** (Isaiah 53:6a LXX). Our selfish motives tend to crowd out the Word of God, forcing His will from our hearts and minds. One day we wake up wondering why God feels so distant. It is because we have laid down the Bible, and are treading blindly down an aimless path, going with the flow, forgetting that **wide is the gate, and broad is the way, that leads to destruction, and many there be which go in thereat** (Matthew 7:13b). God is faithful, providing us with all the wisdom and direction we need through His Word; but we have been unfaithful, seeking answers to our questions from the world. Such answers are empty and godless counterfeits: **This wisdom descendeth not from above, but is earthly, sensual[4], devilish** (James 3:15).

---

[2]   In anthropological discourse, the "Self", along with its notions, perceptions, affections, and lusts, has been deified so that ultimately, our preoccupation with it has become a form of self-worship, which is idolatry. In this book, the term means "ego" or "flesh". It refers to all actions made selfishly, or "in the flesh".

[3]   www.dictionaryreference.com

[4]   That is, of the flesh. Desires of the flesh are not limited to sexual lusts, as is sometimes assumed. The desires of the flesh are the desires of this world—the distractions of the heart and mind that are ungodly or unfruitful, that lead us away from Christ. "…abstain from fleshly lusts, which war against the soul" 1 Peter 2:11. See also James 4:1-5.

Jesus Christ has graciously provided us with the perfect example for us to live by in His Word. **Forasmuch then as Christ hath suffered for us in the flesh, arm yourselves likewise with the same mind: for he that hath suffered in the flesh hath ceased from sin; That he no longer should live the rest of his time in the flesh to the lusts of men, but to the will of God** (1 Peter 4:1-2). Obedience must be learned and it is learned through suffering (Hebrews 5:8-9). We suffer when we deny our Self (our flesh or ego), to do the will of God. For Jesus and for countless others, this denial of Self meant tribulation and death. Paul wrote that **no man should be moved by these afflictions: for yourselves know that we are appointed thereunto** (1 Thessalonians 3:3).

Our God of love appoints us to be afflicted and chastens us **for our profit, that we might be partakers of his holiness** (Hebrews 12:10b). When we are "exercised" by God in this manner, we are to endure with joy (James 1:2), knowing that our afflictions are wrought for His glory and our profit. **Now no chastening for the present seemeth to be joyous, but grievous: nevertheless afterward it yieldeth the peaceable fruit of righteousness unto them which are exercised thereby** (Hebrews 12:11).

Remember and be comforted by the fact that only those whom the Lord loves, He chastens.[5] The difficulty we face as His children is proof of our heavenly citizenship (Hebrews 12:7-8). In this we can rejoice. Despite the discomfort, despite the pain, and despite the frustration we may encounter, the end result is that we are made unshakeable. We become the inheritors of an immoveable kingdom (Hebrews 12:28). Therefore, as children of the promise, **we may boldly say, The Lord is my helper, and I will not fear what man shall do unto me** (Hebrews 13:6).

If you lay down your Self at the feet of the Lord as a **living sacrifice** (Romans 12:1b), you will be ready to learn what He leads you to see through the following examples. Be not afraid of His chastisement. When you accept His instruction and persevere to learn from it, He will bless and prosper your soul (3 John 1:2).

---

5   Proverbs 3:12 LXX, Hebrews 12:6, Revelation 3:19.

Profile #1: The Foolish Woman
Thou Hast Done Foolishly (2 Chronicles 16:9 LXX)
JOB'S WIFE

We have all heard the story of Job, but what do we know about Job's wife? We meet her in the second chapter of Job. At this point, all of Job's possessions had been destroyed and his children killed. When the devil returned to the presence of God, after completing his vile mission, God said to him for the second time, **Hast thou then observed my servant Job, that there is none of men upon the earth like him, a harmless, true, blameless, godly man, abstaining from all evil? and he yet cleaves to innocence, whereas thou hast told me to destroy his substance without cause?** (Job 2:3 LXX).

Clearly Job's wife was married to a godly and upright man. Her husband feared God, and he put evil away from himself (eschewed evil) continually. Despite having experienced the dreaded pain of having lost all his children, Job remained godly, and held fast his integrity. Instead of cursing God, he blessed His name: **In all these events that befell him Job sinned not at all before the Lord, and did not impute folly to God** (Job 1:22 LXX). When calamity came upon him, he knew better than to blame God.

In Job 2:6, the devil was given permission by God to take away Job's health, but not his life. The devil immediately went and **smote Job with sore boils from his feet to his head. And he took a potsherd to scrape away the discharge, and sat upon a dung-heap outside the city** (Job 2:7-8 LXX). Job must have looked like quite a sorry mess. At this moment, his wife had an opportunity to minister to him. She could have anointed him with oil, prayed for him, placed a compress against his wounds, or given him a cool drink. She could have offered him some words of encouragement or consolation. But she did not. Instead, she said to him:

> **How long wilt thou hold out, saying, Behold, I wait yet a little while, expecting the hope of my deliverance? for, behold, thy memorial is abolished from the earth, even thy sons and daughters, the pangs and pains of my womb which I bore in vain with sorrows; and thou thyself sittest down**

to spend the nights in the open air among the corruption of worms, and I am a wanderer and a servant from place to place and house to house, waiting for the setting of the sun, that I may rest from my labours and my pangs which now beset me: but say some word against the Lord, and die (Job 2:9 LXX). [6]

Job's wife was speaking the words of a fool. She was working against an innocent husband, contrary to the will of God. How did the blameless Job respond? **But he looked on her, and said to her, Thou hast spoken like one of the foolish women. If we have received good things of the hand of the Lord, shall we not endure evil things? In all these things that happened to him, Job sinned not at all with his lips before God** (Job 2:10 LXX).

How Does a Woman Display Foolishness?

To be foolish is to lack good sense or judgment.[7] Biblically, a fool is defined as one who behaves hastily, making irrational decisions which reflect deficient foresight. Her lack of discernment and inability to judge righteously (John 7:24) is a direct result of her ignorance of the things of God.[8] A fool can be well-informed in the ways of the world, but she neither knows nor understands the ways of God. She is **Ever learning, and never able to come to the knowledge of the truth** (2 Timothy 3:7).

It is important to note that Job's wife spoke *like* a foolish woman (Job 2:10 LXX). Job was not calling her a fool, but chastising her for sounding like one. The distinction is this. While some of us behave foolishly from time to time, we recognize our mistakes and learn from them.[9] The fool does

---

[6]   This verse in other Bible versions reads simply, "Then said his wife unto him, Dost thou still retain thine integrity? curse God, and die".

[7]   *The Oxford English Reference Dictionary*

[8]   Psalm 14:1 LXX, Jeremiah 4:22, 5:4 LXX, Romans 1:21

[9]   Exemplified by King David in 2 Samuel 24:10 LXX: "And the heart of David smote him after he numbered the people; and David said to the Lord, I have sinned grievously, O Lord, in what I have done: remove, I pray thee, the iniquity of thy servant, for I have been exceedingly foolish".

not. She is defined by her illogical tendency to repeat mistakes (Proverbs 26:11 LXX). For this reason, the Bible identifies the fool as unregenerate[10] (Proverbs 24:9 LXX) and evil (Proverbs 14:33 LXX). By learning from her mistakes, we can avoid making them.

The story of Job's wife provides us with a departure point from which we can identify the following traits of foolishness: 1) she is reactive, 2) she is deceived, 3) she reproaches the Lord, 4) she is self-destructive, and 5) she devises evil.

1) She is reactive.

It is a glory for a man to turn aside from railing;[11] **but every fool is entangled with such matters** (Proverbs 20:3 LXX). Job's wife had much to grieve over, to be sure; however, complaining and grieving are two very different things. Complaining is a verbal venting of emotional distress that arises out of self-pity. Grief is a feeling of keen sorrow or regret that arises from a great personal loss. A grieving Christian seeks and receives solace from the only true source of solace: the Lord. Job's wife wallowed in self-pity, which culminated in a vocal outburst of self-pity. The result was that she railed at her husband. **Righteous lips cover enmity; but they that utter railings are most foolish** (Proverbs 10:18b LXX).

When a fool speaks, she lacks restraint and discretion. **A fool utters all his mind; but the wise reserves his in part** (Proverbs 29:11 LXX). She is hasty and rash. **The wise will hide discretion; but the mouth of the hasty draws near to ruin** (Proverbs 10:14b LXX). She is quick to speak and slow to think; she **multiplies words** (Ecclesiastes 7:14a LXX) with **an unguarded mouth** (Proverbs 26:28b LXX). The words of a fool catch her up in her own calamity: **A fool's mouth is ruin to him, and his lips are a snare to his soul** (Proverbs 18:7 LXX).

Like the false prophets, who **speak from their own heart** (Jeremiah 23:16 LXX), the **hearts of the foolish are not safe** (Proverbs 15:7b LXX). The fool, boldly following her own heart (Proverbs 28:26 LXX), which is like the heart of a child (Proverbs 22:15 LXX) walking in its own lusts

---

[10] i.e., lost

[11] A railing is a "bitter complaint". www.dictionary.reference.com

(Jeremiah 16:12 LXX), **is led by folly** (Proverbs 18:2b LXX). She does not check the "imaginations of her heart"[12] against the logic of the Word. **The ways of fools are right in their own eyes** (Proverbs 12:15 LXX). Therefore **all things are adverse to a foolish man** (Proverbs 14:7 LXX).

A fool is quick to anger. **Be not hasty in thy spirit to be angry: for anger will rest in the bosom of fools** (Ecclesiastes 7:9 LXX). When anger is left unchecked, the foolish woman will erroneously convince herself that her anger is "justified". Then, she rashly emboldens herself to speak out. What she says will be an embarrassing revelation of what lies in her heart. **A stone is heavy, and sand cumbersome; but a fool's wrath is heavier than both** (Proverbs 27:3 LXX).

STUDY BREAK[13]
Unrighteous Anger

A man slow to wrath abounds in wisdom (Proverbs 14:29a LXX). One day while visiting a church, I witnessed an alarming spectacle. After the service, while the pastor stood at the back door, a woman with a red face full of rage clenched her fists and exclaimed to him, "I was righteously angry!" **The wrath of man worketh not the righteousness of God** (James 1:20).

The wrath of men and women is never righteous and never godly. It is carnal—a work of the flesh (Galatians 5:20). We are told to **Cease from anger, and forsake wrath: fret not thyself so as to do evil** (Psalm 37:8 LXX). Anger is evil and destructive; to provoke it is to sin against our own souls (Proverbs 20:2 LXX).

For how shall a mortal man be just before the Lord? (Job 9:2b LXX). In anger, Jezebel threatened to avenge the deaths of the priests of Baal by murdering Elijah, the prophet of God (1 Kings 19). In anger, Herodias arranged for John the Baptist's head to be brought to her in a

---

[12] God pronounced judgment on the disobedient and unrepentant because "the imagination of man is intently bent upon evil things from his youth" Genesis 8:21 LXX. In Jeremiah 3:17 LXX, God said, "and they shall not walk any more after the imaginations of their evil heart".

[13] A "Study Break" is not a break *from* study; it's a break *to* study!

charger (Matthew 14). In anger, Saul threw a javelin at young David's head (1 Samuel 19:9). In anger, the Pharisees took up stones, forced Stephen from the city gates, and murdered him (Acts 7). God said, **I will not act according to the fury of my wrath . . . for I am God, and not man** (Ezekiel 11:9 LXX).

There is only One who is perfectly just in His anger. He is God: **a consuming fire** (Hebrews 12:29). He is storing up wrath against the children of disobedience (Ephesians 5:6), and will pour it out on them in the last days (Revelation 16:1). Until that time, He is **not willing that any should perish** (2 Peter 3:9) because **His mercy endures forever** (Psalm 106:1 LXX). His wrath is in equal proportion to His mercy because He is just. We are not.

We must be ever so careful that in our so-called "righteous" anger, we do not lose sight of who we are. We are those who are under grace (Romans 6:15). While in **the body of this death** (Romans 7:24), our righteousness is fleeting and not yet eternal. Therefore we cannot, nor may we force righteousness on a fallen world until we are **having in a readiness to revenge all disobedience, when your obedience is fulfilled** (2 Corinthians 10:6). Our obedience will be fulfilled when we return in our heavenly bodies with Christ (Revelation 19:14). We will be His army, eliciting judgment and punishment for the sins of the world (Revelation 19:15). Until then, only God can be justifiably angry.

While on this earth, we are to leave vengeance to God: **Dearly beloved, avenge not yourselves, but rather give place unto wrath: for it is written, Vengeance is mine; I will repay, saith the Lord** (Romans 12:19). When we give "place" to wrath, we are giving it over to whom it belongs. It belongs to God. When we allow it to fester within us, we are giving in to a satanic influence. Paul wrote, **Be ye angry, and sin not: let not the sun go down upon your wrath: Neither give place to the devil** (Ephesians 4:26-27). The "place" being referred to in this verse is a foothold or an invitation. "Be ye angry" is not an imperative or command. It is an acknowledgment of the state we sometimes find ourselves in. Paul's meaning is clear: Christians must restrain themselves from being angry or wrathful (Ephesians 4:31).

For example, when Jesus was turned away from a Samaritan village, James and John sought revenge on the "inhospitable" Samaritans. James and John said, **Lord, wilt thou that we command fire to come down from heaven, and consume them, even as Elias did?** (Luke 9:54). Their desire for revenge was ungodly and unjust. It arose out of a spirit of anger, which is not of the Lord. Jesus **turned, and rebuked them, and said, Ye know not what manner of spirit ye are of. For the Son of man is not come to destroy men's lives, but to save them** (Luke 9:55-56a). As fellow-labourers of Jesus Christ while on this earth, we are to assist in His efforts to save the lost. Because we do not strive against people, but against evil spirits (Ephesians 6:12), our love for people must inspire our Christian witness, not our wrath.

Sometimes what we mistake for "righteous anger" is a desire for justice. We all yearn for justice because we live in an unjust world. King David wrote **the torrents of ungodliness troubled me exceedingly** (Psalm 18:4b LXX). The apostle Peter wrote of Lot: **For that righteous man dwelling among [the wicked], in seeing and hearing, vexed his righteous soul from day to day with their unlawful deeds** (2 Peter 2:8). Wickedness grieves the soul of the righteous. It does not compel them to act in anger or hatred.

David writes, **fret not thyself because of him that prospers in his way, at the man that does unlawful deeds** (Psalm 37:7b LXX). When we allow injustice to upset or anger us, we have forgotten that God is in control, and that we must faithfully wait on His judgment. **For evil-doers shall be destroyed: but they that wait on the Lord, they shall inherit the land** (Psalm 37:9 LXX). By waiting on the Lord, we will see injustice requited and evil destroyed—fully and finally (Psalm 92:7 LXX).

It is a fearful thing to fall into the hands of the living God (Hebrews 10:31). The wise, Solomon says, are sorrowful as a result of understanding this. **The heart of the wise is in the house of mourning; but the heart of fools is in the house of mirth** (Ecclesiastes 7:4 LXX). The wise are burdened by the sin that is in the world and are sobered by the imminent destruction of the wicked. They will wait on the Lord's justice and they will be filled. Until then, we are to show judgment with mercy (James 2:13) as children of peace (Matthew 5:9), not of wrath (1 Thessalonians 5:9).

Job's wife did not rely on God in faith to actualize His plans. Her impatience and near-sightedness caused her to lash out in anger against a faultless husband and a Holy God. When you are struggling to understand

God's purpose for things that happen in your life, **Be still, and know that [the Lord is] God** (Psalm 46:10a LXX). Then, **Wait on the Lord** (Psalm 37:34a LXX).

2) She is deceived.

A foolish woman fails to connect cause with effect and is therefore easily misled. **The law of the wise is a fountain of life: but the man void of understanding shall die by a snare** (Proverbs 13:14 LXX). She fails to see reason: **The ways of a foolish man are void of sense; but a wise man proceeds on his way aright** (Proverbs 15:21 LXX). Although there is danger all around her, she does not heed the warnings: **A wise man, when evils are approaching, hides himself; but fools pass on, and will be punished** (Proverbs 27:12 LXX).

The fool walks headlong into disaster—repeatedly. **A threat breaks down the heart of a wise man; but a fool, though scourged, understands not** (Proverbs 16:16 LXX). A fool arrogantly relies on her own "wisdom" and therefore is witlessly enveloped by evil. **A wise man fears, and departs from evil; but the fool trusts in himself, and joins himself with the transgressor** (Proverbs 14:16 LXX).

A fool does not follow the admonition to **Prove all things; hold fast to that which is good** (1 Thessalonians 5:21). She **believes every word: but the prudent man betakes himself to after-thought** (Proverbs 14:15 LXX). As a result, she gets caught up in vain philosophies (2 Peter 2:18), lacking the understanding to identify falsehood and lacking the humility to mind a timely warning.

For example, postmodernist philosophy has rendered truth subjective. In other words, whatever someone believes to be true is true for that person, even though someone else may believe the opposite. A Christian's grasp of truth is God-centred, focused on the Biblical reality, which contains the infallible, unchanging record of God's sovereign existence. A foolish Christian will agree that truth is subjective, not realizing that by so doing, she invalidates her faith by professing that her belief in God is her subjective truth, relevant only for her. **Strong delusion** (2 Thessalonians 2:11a) has come upon her; she is **deceiving, and being deceived** (2 Timothy 3:13).

With God, there is no confusion. All is foreknown, foreordained, and predestined. There is certainty at every turn. This confidence, which breeds integrity, escapes the fool, and she neither sees nor foresees God's truth. She is **carried about by every wind of doctrine** (Ephesians 4:14b). As a result, she is an incompetent, nominal Christian who fails as a witness of Christ, who neither serves nor glorifies God in the truth.

Let no man deceive himself. If any man among you seemeth to be wise in this world, let him become a fool, that he may be wise (1 Corinthians 3:18). Intellectual standards set by secular, higher education and media are cheap, satanic counterfeits. They are idols that millions of North Americans bend the knee to daily. Christians who become enamoured by them invariably lose their grasp on truth. When truth is lost, reason is not far behind. **Be not deceived; God is not mocked: for whatsoever a man soweth, that shall he also reap** (Galatians 6:7). Build your house on the firm foundation of the truth of Christ by removing the influences of the world. Only then will you be able to see clearly enough to recognize truth and avoid deception.

Job's wife misjudged his situation because her understanding was based on worldly wisdom. Like his friends, she assumed that life on this earth was supposed to be fair and that bad things happen to sinful people. This is not what the Bible teaches. The sun rises and sets on the good and evil, just as the rain falls on them both (Matthew 5:45). Justice will not come to this earth until the Lord Jesus Christ brings it upon His return.

Until that great and glorious day, we are to live in this present, unfair, and fallen world under heavenly appointment to suffer and endure hardships.[14] The way we react to them reveals our hearts: **Yet if any man suffer as a Christian, let him not be ashamed; but let him glorify God on this behalf** (1 Peter 4:16). How do you react when things aren't going your way? Do you interpret your situation with godly wisdom, or with the foolishness of this world? Instead of glorifying God in the midst of her adversity, instead of enduring with patience the race that was set before her, Job's wife demanded justice from an unjust world. She was deceived.

---

[14] 1 John 3:13, 1 Peter 4:19, John 15:19-20

3) She reproaches the Lord.

There are three ways that a fool reproaches the Lord. One is to find fault with Him. **Arise, O God, plead thy cause: remember thy reproaches that come from the foolish one all the day** (Psalm 74:22 LXX). A fool brings an accusation against the Almighty God. She hastily blames Him for the difficulties she encounters. **The folly of a man spoils his ways: and he blames God in his heart** (Proverbs 19:3 LXX). Job was no fool: **In all these events that befell him Job sinned not at all before the Lord, and did not impute folly to God** (Job 1:22 LXX).

Remarkably, but not coincidentally, Job's exemplary response is mirrored in the New Testament experience of the early church: **But and if ye suffer for righteousness' sake, happy are ye: and be not afraid of their terror, neither be troubled; But sanctify the Lord God in your hearts** (1 Peter 3:14-15). To sanctify is to cleanse, make holy, or hold guiltless. When we suffer, we are to hold God inviolate, reverencing Him with thankfulness, resisting the temptation to feel anger against Him for our pain. A fool does not see pain as an opportunity for grace to abound; she uses it as an excuse to cry foul. She accuses the Lord of mistreatment or abuse. By violating the holiness of God and profaning His name, she is guilty of reproaching Him. **If we have received good things of the hand of the Lord, shall we not endure evil things?** (Job 2:10b LXX).

The second way to reproach the Lord is to blaspheme His Name, or His Word. Blasphemy is a reproach taken one step too far. To blaspheme the Lord is to speak evil of Him. This is no small matter. In the Old Testament example of Eli, the high priest, and his two errant sons, Hophni and Phinehas, God communicates to us exactly how He feels about those who speak evil of Him. He said to Samuel, **And I have told [Eli] that I will be avenged on his house perpetually for the iniquities of his sons, because his sons spoke evil against God, and he did not admonish them** (1 Samuel 3:13 LXX). God told Samuel that there could be no atonement[15] for the sins of Hophni and Phinehas (1 Samuel 3:14 LXX). Fools speak evil of God.

---

[15] If you have committed the sin of blasphemy in ignorance, you can be forgiven. Numbers 15:28 LXX, "And the priest shall make atonement for the soul that committed the trespass unwillingly, and that sinned unwillingly before the

A fool also speaks evil of the Word of God. **In the beginning was the Word, and the Word was with God, and the Word was God** (John 1:1). When a believer has the Word of God available to her and holds it in low regard, she is holding God in low regard. **And he was clothed with a vesture dipped in blood: and his name is called The Word of God** (Revelation 19:13). She who resists taking instruction from the Word resists taking instruction from God. **All scripture is given by inspiration of God** (2 Timothy 3:16a); **holy men of God spake as they were moved by the Holy Ghost** (2 Peter 1:21b). By casting off the Word as irrelevant, out-dated, inconvenient, or unreliable, she blasphemes the Word of God. She speaks evil of it, and brings a reproach against its Author (Titus 2:5).

The third way a fool reproaches God is by giving His enemies cause to accuse Him. **An enemy has reproached the Lord, and a foolish people has provoked thy name** (Psalm 74:18b LXX). When the children of God sin and are unrepentant, they are punished. **For they hated wisdom, and did not choose the word of the Lord: neither would they attend to my counsels, but derided my reproofs. Therefore shall they eat the fruits of their own way, and shall be filled with their own ungodliness** (Proverbs 1:29-31 LXX).

A Christian under punishment is "eating the fruits of her own way". In other words, she is left to the natural consequences of her sin. From a failed marriage to rebellious children, depression, illness, or futility, her life paints a highly negative picture of what it is to be a Christian.

Please note that I am talking specifically about a Christian woman who is under punishment for sin. I am not talking about the calamities of life in a fallen world. Not all women who suffer are being punished by God any more than Job was. The blind man healed by Jesus was not under punishment because of his sins or the sins of his parents, but was blind so that **the works of God should be made manifest in him** (John 9:3). Similarly, some women are suffering so that God's strength can be made perfect in them (2 Corinthians 12:9). Their suffering is not their "fault"; it is an opportunity for them to rely fully on God.

Lord, to make atonement for him". In 1 Timothy 1:13 Paul wrote of himself, "Who was before a blasphemer, and a persecutor, and injurious: but I obtained mercy, because I did it ignorantly in unbelief".

For a Christian who is suffering as a consequence of sin, her undesirable life experiences depict Christianity as something to be sneered at. A sullen, ornery, joyless woman often does Christianity irreparable damage and disservice. Unless her circumstances improve and she accredits positive changes to the grace and glory of God, He will be held responsible for the poor quality of her life.

Give none occasion to the adversary to speak reproachfully (1 Timothy 5:14). The adversary cannot open his mouth in reproach when we obey the Word of God and experience the fruits of righteousness. Good fruit makes Christianity look both desirable and fulfilling, bringing glory to God. **A good man out of the good treasure of the heart bringeth forth good things** (Matthew 12:35a). The good things that you bring forth as a Christian are the fruits of the Spirit: **love, joy, peace, longsuffering, gentleness, goodness, faith, Meekness, temperance** (Galatians 5:22-23a). All of these traits are observable proofs of your heavenly citizenship. All **adorn the doctrine of God our Saviour** (Titus 2:10a).

Job's wife said to him, **but say some word against the Lord, and die** (Job 2:9 LXX). The King James Version (KJV) reads, **curse God, and die**. Blasphemy is the unforgiveable sin (Mark 3:29). Like "suicide by cop", when someone intentionally compels the police to react with lethal force, killing him or her, Job was advised by his own wife to kill himself by compelling a similar reaction from the Almighty God.

4) She is self-destructive.

Wise women build houses: but a foolish one digs hers down with her hands (Proverbs 14:1 LXX). A foolish woman does not build her house upon the rock by heeding the commandments of Christ. Her home is built on sand: **And every one that heareth these sayings of mine, and doeth them not, shall be likened unto a foolish man, which built his house upon the sand** (Matthew 7:26). A house built on sand cannot stand. It will fall.

Jesus likens a house built upon solid rock as one whose builder is wise—a man who hears the sayings of Christ and does them (Matthew 7:24). The foolish one whose house is built upon the sand resists instruction and hates the knowledge that comes from Christ. **And the rain descended, and the floods came, and the winds blew, and beat upon that house; and it fell: and great was the fall of it** (Matthew 7:27).

He that loves instruction loves sense, but he that hates reproofs is a fool (Proverbs 12:1 LXX). A foolish woman refuses to learn either from God or from the godly. She is willingly ignorant (2 Peter 3:5), tearing down that which needs to be built up. Too ignoble to build her house upon that which is greater than herself, the fool has erected a weak structure based on the **wisdom of this world** (1 Corinthians 3:19) and wonders why it keeps falling down. The path of fools ends in destruction: her **bold mouth calls for death** (Proverbs 18:6b LXX).

5) She devises evil.

They that go astray devise evils: but the good devise mercy and truth (Proverbs 14:22 LXX). The fool goes astray from the path of righteousness and lives contrary to the will of God. Because she is perpetually on the wrong path, **the occupation of fools is evil** (Proverbs 14:24 LXX). She brings evil on both herself and on others.

A foolish man digs up evil for himself (Proverbs 16:27b LXX). Because she lacks discernment, she mistakes evil for good. She confuses the bitterness of rebellion for the sweet savour of self-sacrifice. **He that pronounces the unjust just, and the just unjust is unclean and abominable with God** (Proverbs 17:15 LXX). She eschews good and embraces evil. Whether she is cognizant of her folly or not, she is repeating the actions of the original rebel.

A fool brings evil on others. If you have a fool for a friend, be warned. **The instruction of fools is evil** (Proverbs 16:22b LXX). She lacks discernment in every area, from choosing to wear an immodest dress to choosing to serve a self-fashioned god. Her instruction is not just misguided, it is iniquitous. There is nothing to be gained from having a fool for a friend. **If thou walkest with wise men thou shalt be wise: but he that walks with fools shall be known** (Proverbs 13:20 LXX).

It is better to identify a fool as such and leave her influence than it is to remain by her side and enable her. **Go not in the ways of the ungodly,**

neither covet the ways of transgressors. In whatever place they shall pitch their camp, go not thither; but turn from them, and pass away (Proverbs 4:14-15 LXX). Jumping into a ditch alongside her will not help her get out.

Shame and dishonour mark the fool. Do not be like her. **The heart of a fool is grief to its possessor** (Proverbs 17:21 LXX).

Modern Snapshot[16]
CINDY

Cindy was raised in a double-income Christian home. She was taught from a young age to be assertive and out-going. As a teen, she spent time as a missionary in Venezuela. In order to fit in with their cultural practices, she wore a thong bikini bottom and went topless on their beaches. She considered this to be an important bonding practice, and felt proud to have accomplished it without feeling shame.

Cindy married a good, Christian boy who was home-schooled. In her wedding speech, she said that she married him because he was the first to ask. Considering him naïve and inexperienced, she took it upon herself to teach him what he needed to know. Out of respect for her "spirituality" and "wisdom", he allowed her to make all the child-rearing decisions in their home.

After being warned of the dangers of vaccines, Cindy conducted her own research on the matter at her local library. Concluding that modern medicine could not be wrong, she chose to vaccinate her children. Although they were prone to viral infections, asthma, and were fraught with various allergies, immuno-deficiencies, and behavioural disorders, she saw no connection between their health and the vaccines.

From an early age, Cindy's children were not trained in the way they should go. When they inevitably manifested negative, selfish behaviour, they were not chastised. Cindy believed that leaving children to express

---

[16] Each Modern Snapshot is based on a real person whose character and life experience contain similarities to the profiles given in each chapter of this book. These are meant for instructional purposes only. Names and details have been changed to protect privacy.

themselves in various forms uninterrupted was essential to their learning process. When she sent her oldest to public school, she said that she wanted him to be a "light shining in a world of darkness". This "light" bullied many "friends", along with their mothers, who warned Cindy about her son's behaviour to no avail. Out of consternation, unwilling to admit her mistakes, she had her son diagnosed with ADD, and he is currently a medicated, "Christian", eight-year-old.

Cindy has found so much "success" with child-raising, that she is hoping to foster or adopt more children into her home. She prefers to work outside the home several days a week, and although she is a full-time mom in between, she cannot care for both of her children at the same time. Her husband makes the necessary childcare arrangements to accommodate her needs.

Cindy believes what is reported in the media. She has taken several female empowerment courses and has read related books. She has come to realize that God is a woman. No one needs to believe her, of course, but she "knows" this to be true. To Cindy, any man who expects obedience from his wife is a misogynist[17] and any woman who serves her husband willingly is a fool. She attends a Christian church, and considers herself to be a righteous and moral example of a typical, modern, "Christian" mother.

Honour is not seemly for a fool (Proverbs 26:1 LXX).

Summary

Willingly ignorant, unable to see far off, the fool is ensnared by her own folly. She is emotionally unstable, subject to punishment, deceived, unlearned, blasphemous, and in danger of judgment. The greatest challenge facing the fool is for her to admit that she is one. She is blinded by her pride: **but the foolish being lovers of haughtiness, having become ungodly have hated knowledge, and are become subject to reproofs** (Proverbs 1:22 LXX).

The only way for a fool to recognize her folly is through reproof. If you have read this chapter and identified yourself as being in some ways foolish,

---

[17]   Woman-hater

then you have accepted admonition and chosen to learn from God's Word. Out of humility, you have bent your will to the Lord's. If this is true of you, then by definition, you are no longer foolish! The good Lord can work miracles in a repentant heart, but He will do little with a hardened one.

All of us were once fools and may continue to be from time to time. A few of my favourite verses about this are the following:

> **For we ourselves also were sometimes foolish, disobedient, deceived, serving divers lusts and pleasures, living in malice and envy, hateful, and hating one another. But after that the kindness and love of God our Saviour toward man appeared, Not by works of righteousness which we have done, but according to his mercy he saved us, by the washing of regeneration, and renewing of the Holy Ghost; Which he shed on us abundantly through Jesus Christ our Saviour; That being justified by his grace, we should be made heirs according to the hope of eternal life** (Titus 3:3-7).

These verses tell the story of the Christian's life—so short, so sweet, and so poignant. Look at the wording in verse 4: **the kindness and love of God our Saviour toward man appeared**. It appeared. The blind cannot see it. Those who are not called in Christ cannot see it. The proud, haughty, and unregenerate cannot see it. But it will appear to those who seek it.

> **And I will devise for you a device of peace, and not evil, to bestow upon you these good things. And do ye pray to me, and I will hearken to you: and do ye earnestly seek me, and ye shall find me; for ye shall seek me with your whole heart. And I will appear to you** (Jeremiah 36:11-14 LXX).

God, in His mercy, has offered to remove our blinders and permit us to see. Look for Him, and He will appear before you, majestic and true, in all kindness and love, inviting you into His kingdom. Will you come?

Who Shall Deliver Me?

Since I called, and ye did not hearken; and I spoke at length, and ye gave no heed; but ye set at nought my counsels, and disregarded my reproofs; therefore I also will laugh at your destruction; and I will rejoice against you when ruin comes upon you: yea when dismay suddenly comes upon you, and your overthrow shall arrive like a tempest; and when tribulation and distress shall come upon you, or when ruin shall come upon you.

For it shall be that when ye call upon me, I will not hearken to you: wicked men shall seek me, but shall not find me. For they hated wisdom, and did not choose the word of the Lord: neither would they attend to my counsels, but derided my reproofs. Therefore shall they eat the fruits of their own way, and shall be filled with their own ungodliness. For because they wronged the simple, they shall be slain; and an inquisition shall ruin the ungodly. But he that hearkens to me shall dwell in confidence, and shall rest securely from all evil (Proverbs 1:24-33 LXX).

- For God hath not appointed us to wrath, but to obtain salvation by our Lord Jesus Christ (1 Thessalonians 5:9).
- Ye are of God, little children, and have overcome [every spirit that confesseth not that Jesus Christ is come in the flesh]: because greater is he that is in you, than he that is in the world (1 John 4:4).

How Can I be Wise?

1. Seek instruction from God's Word (2 Timothy 3:16-17).
2. Accept instruction (1 Corinthians 10:11-12, Proverbs 12:1 LXX).
3. Speak less (Matthew 15:11, James 1:19.)
4. Listen more (Proverbs 14:15 LXX, Proverbs 16:17 LXX).
5. Fear the Lord (Proverbs 1:7 LXX).
6. Depart from evil (Proverbs 3:7 LXX).
7. Seek the company of the wise (Proverbs 13:20 LXX).

Think on These Things

1. *How can I become a child of God?*
   John 1:12

2. *How can I become righteous?*
   John 1:29, John 1:9

3. *How can I make time to read God's word each day?*
   Rom. 13:12, Deut. 8:3

4. *How can I use my words to build up my family in Christ?*
   Rom. 15:13

5. *How can I make my life more peaceful?*
   Rom. 12:21

6. *How can I do what God wants?*
   Rom. 8:11

7. *Why is there evil?*
   Rom. 5:12

8. *How can I get through trials?*
   1 Peter 3:14-15

9. *How can I show more respect to my husband?*
   Prov. 14:22

10. *What is my place in the world?*
    Psalm 8:3-6

CHAPTER TWO

THE HARD OF HEART

PROVERBS 28:14 LXX

STUDY BREAK
The Heart

Before beginning this chapter, I did a word-search for "heart" in the King James Bible. It appears 884 times. What I found is condensed in the following paragraphs. Due to the length, I will not footnote each reference. Search any of the key words or phrases, and you will find the reference in the King James Bible. References from the Septuagint will be noted.

Out of the heart, we think, speak, and act. We feel, grieve, lament, and despise with our hearts. Our hearts smite us, they tremble, they fear, they pant, they plague, they break, and they faint. Hearts can be destroyed. They die. They can turn away from someone or incline towards someone. One heart can be knit to another. They inspire us to give, to serve, to be good, to be honest, and to be perfect. Hearts can be kept or stolen. They can be subtle, froward,[1] privy to wickedness, lustful, and perverse. Hearts can be wise or foolish. They understand and know. They can be proud, haughty, or lowly. Hearts can be merry. Hearts can be full of joy and gladness. They can rejoice.

---

[1] Froward means "wilfully contrary" according to www.dictionaryreference.com

Hearts can be troubled, desolate, pained, or contrite. They can err or backslide. They can be moved, set, fixed, established, brought down, lifted up, or carried away. They can be overwhelmed.

Like wax, hearts can melt. Like milk, hearts can curdle.[2] Hearts can be enlarged, slow, hardened, or gross.[3] Hearts can be offended or made tender. Hearts search, find, and follow. Hearts can deceive and be deceived. Hearts can prepare to seek the Lord. They can both sow and conceive. Hearts can be strengthened. Hearts can be valiant, righteous, and have integrity. Hearts can be insatiable, hateful, hypocritical, or worthless. Hearts can be trusting, blameless, and faithful. They can love. Out of the heart proceed evil thoughts, murders, adulteries, fornications, thefts, false witness, and blasphemies.

Hearts can be pure and clean. Hearts can be mad or they can be sound.[4] Hearts can frame things falsely or be mischievous. They can be proved and tried. They can be determined and emboldened. Both evil and forgiveness come from the heart. Hearts can imagine things, ponder things, and doubt things. The commandments of the Lord can be kept, written, placed, and bound in the heart. Hearts can discern and counsel. Hearts can be deep or heavy. Hearts envy and strive. Hearts glory and exalt. Hearts can be vexed or hasty. Hearts can be awakened and hearts can be ravished.

A heart can study and guide. A heart can be burned, cut, sprinkled, or pricked. Hearts can be reduced to ashes.[5] They can be purposeful, single, and steadfast. Believers can be of one heart. One can obey from the heart, sorrow in the heart, and believe in the heart. Hearts can treasure up wrath. Hearts can be veiled, hidden, and secretive. Hearts can be afflicted and anguished. Hearts can be blind. With grace, hearts can sing. Hearts can be comforted. Our hearts can condemn us or reproach us. We can sanctify the Lord God in our hearts and our hearts can do the will of God.

---

[2]   Psalm 119:70a in the Septuagint reads, "Their heart has been curdled like milk". In the King James, it says, "Their heart is as fat as grease".

[3]   In Matthew 13:15 and Acts 28:27, quoted from Isaiah 6:10, the heart of the people is "waxed gross". They are "dull of hearing", and their eyes are "closed".

[4]   "Mad" means insane, and "sound", means sane.

[5]   Isaiah 44:20 LXX, "Know thou that their heart is ashes, and they err, and no one is able to deliver his soul..."

The love of God is shed in our hearts. The light of God shines in our hearts. The Spirit of the Son of God dwells in our hearts. The peace of God can rule in our hearts. The day star will arise in our hearts. God can touch your heart and He can change it. He can give you a new heart. He looks on your heart.

The one reference out of the 884 of interest for this chapter is this: A heart can be circumcised (Jeremiah 4:4 LXX). In fact, it must be in order for us to enter the kingdom of heaven.[6]

Profile #2: The Hard-hearted Woman
Who Has Hardened Himself Against [God] and Endured?
(Job 9:4 LXX)
VASHTI

King Artaxerxes was in the third year of his reign as King of Susa. In celebration of his marriage to the beautiful Queen Vashti, he threw an extravagant 180-day feast. Friends, nations, and nobles were all invited. During that time, it was his great pleasure to show them the abundant wealth and glory of his kingdom (Esther 1:4 LXX). Following this feast, the King decided to throw a private, six-day banquet in his own home. **And this banquet was not according to the appointed law; but so the king would have it: and he charged the stewards to perform his will and that of the company** (Esther 1:8 LXX). During this time, Vashti **made a banquet for the women in the palace where king Artaxerxes dwelt** (Esther 1:9 LXX). On the seventh day after the unlawful, six-day feast, "merry" King Artaxerxes told his seven servants to **bring in the queen to him, to enthrone her, and crown her with the diadem, and to shew her to the princes, and her beauty to the nations: for she was beautiful** (Esther 1:11 LXX).

This is the crucial moment in the story. How would the new queen respond to her husband's first command of their marriage? You read the rest of the story:

---

6   Psalm 95:11 LXX, Ezekiel 44:9 LXX

But queen [Vashti] hearkened not to him to come with the chamberlains: so the king was grieved and angered. And he said to his friends, Thus hast [Vashti] spoken: pronounce therefore upon this case law and judgment.

So . . . the princes of the Persians and Medes, who were near the king, who sat chief in rank by the king, drew near to him, and reported to him according to the laws how it was proper to do to queen [Vashti], because she had not done the things commanded of the king by the chamberlains. And [Memucan] said to the king and to the princes, Queen [Vashti] has not wronged the king only, but also all the king's rulers and princes: for he has told them the words of the queen, and how she disobeyed the king.

As then, said he, she refused to obey King Artaxerxes, so this day shall the other ladies of the chiefs of the Persians and Medes, having heard what she said to the king, dare in the same way to dishonour their husbands. If then it seem good to the king, let him make a royal decree, and let it be written according to the laws of the Medes and Persians, and let him not alter it: and let not the queen come in to him any more; and let the king give her royalty to a woman better than she. And let the law of the king which he shall have made, be widely proclaimed, in his kingdom: and so shall all the women give honour to their husbands, from the poor even to the rich.

And the saying pleased the king and the princes; and the king did as [Memucan] had said, and sent into all his kingdom through the several provinces, according to their language, in order that men might be feared in their own **houses** (Esther 1:12-22 LXX paragraph breaks mine).

STUDY BREAK
Queen Vashti

The story of Queen Vashti is rife with Biblical and marital insights. There is much to see and learn from her example which is so indelibly linked to that of Queen Esther.

First, the husband is to the wife as God is to the church (Ephesians 5:23). This is so whether a husband and wife are saved by the blood of Christ or not. King Artaxerxes and Vashti represent this relationship in uncanny ways. For example, the word "hearkened" in the first chapter of the story[7] is the same word God uses for those who "hearken" to His voice, and for those who were to "hearken" to the voices of the prophets. Like the Israelites who **hearkened not** (Psalm 81:11 LXX) to the voice of the Lord, Vashti **hearkened not** (Esther 1:12 LXX) to the voice of her husband.

The King did not come himself to inform her of his bidding. He sent chamberlains. Similarly, the Lord sent prophets to tell the Israelites what was expected of them. Just as Vashti hearkened not to the voice of the chamberlains, the Israelties hearkened not to the voices of the prophets. Like Vashti, who was too busy partying with her girlfriends to do the bidding of her husband, the Israelites were too busy worshiping idols and cavorting with the unclean to obey God.

Artaxerxes was so thrilled with his beautiful wife that he wanted to honour her and bring glory to himself. He wanted to robe her in splendour, crown her, and give her the ornaments of a bride.[8] Similarly, the Lord loves His people. He wants to prosper us, to give us the desires of our heart, and to enthrone us with glory and honour. **Let my soul rejoice in the Lord; for he has clothed me with the robe of salvation, and the garment of joy: he has put a mitre on me as on a bridegroom, and adorned me with ornaments as a bride** (Isaiah 61:10 LXX). As Artaxerxes boasted of Vashti's worth before his friends, so the Lord boasted about his servant Job before His counsel of angels. **Hast thou then observed my servant Job, that there is none of men upon the earth like him, a harmless, true, blameless, godly man, abstaining from all evil?** (Job 2:3 LXX).

Disobedience and rebellion will kindle the Lord's wrath, just as Vashti's disobedience kindled Artaxerxes' anger. **For the Lord said to the children**

---

[7] Esther 1:12 LXX

[8] Some believe that Artaxerxes, in a drunken stupor, demanded that Vashti come to him so that he could disrobe her before all his friends. There is nothing in the text to support this, nor is it the behaviour expected of a successful and powerful Persian king. His heart was "merry", not "sluggish" or "clumsy". There is every reason to believe that he was proud of her and simply wanted to share his joy with his friends.

of Israel, Ye are a stiffnecked people; take heed lest I bring on you another plague, and destroy you: now then put off your glorious apparel, and your ornaments, and I will shew thee what I will do to thee (Exodus 33:5 LXX). Just as Artaxerxes dethroned Vashti, stripping her of her title and rights, taking away her glorious apparel and crown, so will God withhold those things from those who reject Him.

The daughters of Zion rejected Him, so the Lord said that He would

> take away the glory of their raiment, the curls and the fringes and the crescents, and the chains, and the ornaments of their faces, and the array of glorious ornaments, and the armlets, and the bracelets, and the wreathed work, and the finger-rings, and the ornaments for the right hand, and the ear-rings, and the garments with scarlet borders, and the garments with purple grounds, and the shawls to be worn in the house, and the Spartan transparent dresses, and those made of fine linen, and the purple ones, and the scarlet ones, and the fine linen, interwoven with gold and purple, and the light coverings for couches. And there shall be instead of a sweet smell, dust; and instead of a girdle, thou shalt gird thyself with a rope; and instead of a golden ornament for the head, thou shalt have baldness on account of thy works; and instead of a tunic with a scarlet ground, thou shalt gird thyself with sackcloth (Isaiah 3:18-24 LXX).

Vashti was similarly humbled.

King Artaxerxes told his friends, those who sat chief in rank (Esther 1:14 LXX) to him to pronounce therefore upon this case law and judgment (Esther 1:13 LXX). Similarly, the saints and disciples of Christ, who are also His friends, will sit upon thrones of judgment.[9] And Jesus said unto them, Verily I say unto you, that ye which have followed me, in the regeneration when the Son of man shall sit in the throne of his glory, ye also shall sit upon twelve thrones, judging the twelve tribes of Israel (Matthew 19:28).

---

[9] Revelation 20:4, Luke 22:30, 1 Corinthians 6:2-3

King Artaxerxes' decree stated that he would **give [Vashti's] royalty to a woman better than she** (Esther 1:19 LXX). The Israelites were God's chosen people who rebelled against Him, and thereby forfeited their royalty to the Gentiles. **Then Paul and Barnabas waxed bold, and said, It was necessary that the word of God should first have been spoken to you: but seeing ye put it from you, and judge yourselves unworthy of everlasting life, lo, we turn to the Gentiles** (Acts 13:46).

The decrees of King Artaxerxes were published widely, so that all would know his laws and keep them. **And let the law of the king which he shall have made, be widely proclaimed, in his kingdom: and so shall all the women give honour to their husbands, from the poor even to the rich** (Esther 1:20 LXX). Memucan's goal was to publish Vashti's punishment as a negative example, to serve as a warning to the other wives that were in the kingdom. As a result, all women would hear the law and have an opportunity to obey it. **Now all these things happened unto them for ensamples: and are written for our admonition, upon whom the ends of the world are come** (1 Corinthians 10:11).

Paul's exhortation in Colossians reminds us to **be not moved away from the hope of the gospel, which ye have heard, and which was preached to every creature which is under heaven** (Colossians 1:23). All of us have been given the gospel. We all have the opportunity to be baptized into Christ. **For by one Spirit are we all baptized into one body, whether we be Jews or Gentiles, whether we be bond or free; and have been all made to drink into one Spirit** (1 Corinthians 12:13).

The laws of the Medes and Persians could not be altered. Similarly, the laws of the Lord were written by He who has **no variableness, neither shadow of turning** (James 1:17b). King Artaxerxes, anticipating the ramifications of Vashti's rebellion, published a commandment to give other wives in the kingdom every reason to honour their husbands. They would be without excuse if they disobeyed. **And the saying pleased the king and the princes; and the king did as [Memucan] had said, and sent into all his kingdom through the several provinces, according to their language, in order that men might be feared in their own houses** (Esther 1:21-22 LXX).

Similarly, we have the Word of God, published in almost every language on earth, which is able to make us **perfect, thoroughly furnished unto**

all good works (2 Timothy 3:17). If we want our Father in heaven to honour us with the crown of glory, to adorn us with the ornaments of the bride of Christ, and to grant us the inheritance of life eternal with Him, we have just one simple document to read and obey in order to get us there: the Holy Bible.

The Lord has prepared a wedding feast, and has invited everyone to attend; however, only those who are worthy will gain admittance. What makes them worthy? They must be washed by the blood of the Lamb. This is their garment, the appropriate attire for such a feast. In the parable of Matthew 22, a king prepared a wedding for his son, but those he invited would not come. So he said

> **The wedding is ready, but they which were bidden were not worthy. Go ye therefore into the highways, and as many as ye shall find, bid to the marriage . . . . And when the king came in to see the guests, he saw there a man which had not on a wedding garment: And he saith unto him, Friend, how camest thou in hither not having a wedding garment? And he was speechless. Then said the king to the servants, Bind him hand and foot, and take him away, and cast him into outer darkness; there shall be weeping and gnashing of teeth. For many are called, but few are chosen** (Matthew 22:8-9, 11-14).

The parallels to the Vashti story are unmistakeable. Esther wore the appropriate attire, and was granted admittance. Her ornaments were her meek and quiet spirit and her chaste conversation, and with them she won over her unbelieving husband (1 Peter 3:1). Paul said of the wives that they are to wear particular apparel: **Whose adorning let it not be that outward adorning of plaiting the hair, and of wearing of gold, or of putting on of apparel; But let it be the hidden man of the heart, in that which is not corruptible, even the ornament of a meek and quiet spirit, which is in the sight of God of great price** (1 Peter 3:3-4). What are you wearing?

Queen Vashti was beautiful on the outside. She was no doubt lovely beyond measure to behold. However, like the Pharisees whose exterior is clean and righteous and whose interior is filled with **dead men's bones**

(Matthew 23:27b), Queen Vashti's appealing looks could not make up for the ugly, stubborn heart that lay within. When she disobeyed her husband, she revealed herself.

Every woman who reads the Bible has the opportunity to obey it by giving honour to her husband: **and the wife see that she reverence her husband** (Ephesians 5:33b). Every word a woman speaks reveals what lies in her heart, whether she is meek and quiet, or rebellious and obstinate. No matter what you look like on the outside, on the inside do you have the hidden **ornament of a meek and quiet spirit, which is in the sight of God of great price** (1 Peter 3:4)? Please read God's Word, and do what it says.[10] Obey your husband in the Lord, for this is right. **For the eyes of the Lord look upon all the earth, to strengthen every heart that is perfect toward him** (2 Chronicles 16:9a LXX). Reverence and love your *own* husband, and be blessed.

How Does a Woman Harden her Heart?

Biblically, the term "hard of heart" means stubborn. To be stubborn is to be "unreasonably obstinate".[11] A stubborn woman hears correction, recognizes it as needful, but chooses nonetheless to remain in error. The Pharaoh of Moses' time demonstrated the consequences of a hard heart. Although it was clearly unreasonable for him to defy the God of the Hebrews whose power was undeniably both real and unmatched, God hardened his heart so that He could be glorified, and the Egyptian gods defamed. Pharaoh watched his entire kingdom crumble and his army fall as a result of his stubbornness.

A woman who is hard of heart will defiantly watch her marriage and family crumble and fall but will still remain set in her unreasonable ways. Counselling such a woman is a lesson in futility until she opens her heart to the Spirit and will of God.

---

[10] If you want to learn how to honour your husband and make your marriage glorious, I recommend you read Debi Pearl, *Created to be his Help Meet* (Pleasantville, TN: No Greater Joy Ministries, Inc., 2004).

[11] www.dictionary.reference.com

The story of Queen Vashti is instructive in many ways. It draws on several of the deadly sins a hard-hearted wife commits against her husband and against God. As a result, it is imperative that we learn and embrace God's commandments for wives.

It is not enough to know what the Word says on this matter. It is not enough to think about what the Word says on this matter. It is not enough to pray about what the Word says on this matter, nor is it enough to attend a Bible study about what the Word says on this matter. You must *do* what the Word says on this matter: **Therefore as the church is subject unto Christ, so let the wives be to their own husbands in every thing** (Ephesians 5:24). Again, **Wives, submit yourselves unto your own husbands, as it is fit in the Lord** (Colossians 3:18). One more time, with a promise, **Likewise, ye wives, be in subjection to your own husbands; that, if any obey not the word, they also may without the word be won by the conversation of the wives** (1 Peter 3:1).

There is one sure way to receive God's blessings—*do* what the Word of God says. **Blessed are they that hear the word of God, and keep it** (Luke 11:28b). Any literate person can read the Bible, but it takes a woman of wisdom and of substance to do what it says. **If ye love me, keep my commandments** (John 14:15). Is it enough to say you love the Lord? Prove it by doing what He says.

A woman displays stubbornness when she knows what the Lord expects her to do, but does not do it. She will attempt to justify her disobedience in various, creative ways that may seem right to her, **but the end of them looks to the depth of hell** (Proverbs 16:25b LXX). She, like Vashti, whose stubbornness lost her the regency, has 1) an uncircumcised heart, 2) uncircumcised ears, and 3) a stiff neck.

1) An Uncircumcised Heart.

Circumcision was prescribed for the Israelites by God to Abraham in Genesis 17. **And this is the covenant which thou shalt fully keep between me and you, and between thy seed after thee for their generations; every male of you shall be circumcised** (Genesis 17:10 LXX). It was a symbol of the covenant between God and man, a symbol which the Lord considered of utmost importance. **And the uncircumcised male, who shall not be circumcised in the flesh of his foreskin on the eighth day, that soul shall be utterly destroyed from its family, for he has broken my covenant** (Genesis 17:14 LXX).

There is an interesting story about this in Exodus 4:24-26. In a few verses, we are told that when Moses travels from Midian to Egypt to speak to Pharaoh for the first time, he, his wife Zipporah, and his sons stop at an inn. An angel of the Lord meets him there and seeks **to slay him. And [Zipporah] having taken a stone cut off the foreskin of her son, and fell at his feet and said, The blood of the circumcision of my son is staunched:**[12] **and he departed from him** (Exodus 4:24b-26a LXX). Moses had not complied with the Lord's command to circumcise his son, an infraction for which he was held responsible. The angel came to avenge Moses' violation of God's covenant.

Zipporah was not an Israelite, and her father may have counselled Moses against circumcising his son.[13] Nevertheless, they were under this commandment to obey: **And the child of eight days old shall be circumcised by you, every male throughout your generations, and the servant born in the house and he that is bought with money, of every son of a stranger, who is not of thy seed** (Genesis 17:12 LXX). When confronted by the angel, wise Zipporah knew exactly what to do. She performed the circumcision with a stone on the boy who was no longer an infant. She knew that by so doing, the angel would be appeased and Moses' life would be spared. Circumcision was a physical sign of the covenant—a sign of obedience. Where there is obedience, there is no reproach, which is culpability or blame.

Being under reproach is stifling. It is a consequence of being hard of heart. A stifled, guilty heart causes anger and bitterness. When the heart is cleansed of reproach or blame, it is unencumbered and therefore both enabled and encouraged. It is for this reason that fathers are warned: **provoke not your children to anger, lest they be discouraged** (Colossians 3:21).

---

12 The staunching of the blood indicates that the deed had been done, i.e., the blood flow had ceased.

13 The story is told in the *Book of Jasher* 79:8-12. The detail about Moses' father-in-law appears in verse 10.

Discouragement[14] stifles growth. Being uncircumcised of heart is similarly discouraging. It is like carrying around a weight or a burden which diminishes one's ability to believe (Mark 16:14), to understand (John 12:40), to know (Psalm 95:10-11 LXX), and to fear (Isaiah 63:17 LXX) the Lord God.

Conversely, a circumcised heart is free to grow. It is active, productive, and inspired. Like having the burden of guilt removed, the circumcising of the heart removes one's inhibition when it comes to adhering to the will of God. This is true worship: **For we are the circumcision, which worship God in the spirit, and rejoice in Christ Jesus, and have no confidence in the flesh** (Philippians 3:3). It is essential that the flesh of our hearts be circumcised because the flesh represents our fallen, sinful humanity. When the flesh is crucified and the lusts thereof denied, the desires of the flesh dissipate, and a humble, softened heart walks in the spirit, placing all confidence in God.

> **We all had our conversation in times past in the lusts of our flesh, fulfilling the desires of the flesh and of the mind; and were by nature the children of wrath, even as others. But God, who is rich in mercy, for his great love wherewith he loved us, Even when we were dead in sins, hath quickened us together with Christ** (Ephesians 2:3-5a).

Circumcision of the heart does not involve physical cutting. Just as we do not literally ingest the flesh and blood of Jesus Christ when we partake of the Lord's Supper but do so symbolically in remembrance of Him, neither do we need to take a scalpel and carve our hearts. The circumcision of the heart and flesh is a symbolic gesture that reflects our willingness to obey God.

> **And now, Israel, what does the Lord thy God require of thee, but to fear the Lord thy God, and to walk in all his ways, and to love him, and to serve the Lord thy God with all thy heart, and with all thy soul; to keep the commandments of the Lord thy God, and his ordinances, all that I charge thee**

---

[14] "Encourage" is the opposite of "discourage". An encouraged heart is courageous and productive. A discouraged heart is cowardly and immobile.

> to-day, that it may be well with thee? Behold, the heaven
> and the heaven of heavens belong to the Lord thy God, the
> earth and all things that are in it. Only the Lord chose your
> fathers to love them, and he chose out their seed after them,
> even you, beyond all nations, as at this day. Therefore ye
> shall circumcise the hardness of your heart, and ye shall
> not harden your neck (Deuteronomy 10:12-16 LXX).

We, as those whom God has called, have been given the same opportunity as the Israelites have to cut out the hardness of our hearts. We are called to love Him, to serve Him, to walk in His ways, and to keep His commandments. The keeping of His commandments ensures us **that it may be well with thee** (Deuteronomy 10:13 LXX). This promise is extended to the Gentiles, **But he is a Jew, which is one inwardly; and circumcision is that of the heart, in the spirit, and not in the letter; whose praise is not of men, but of God** (Romans 2:29). There is a simple prescription for living well which evades the stubborn heart. It is to obey God.

2) Uncircumcised Ears.

To do the will of God, we must hear His voice. **But my people hearkened not to my voice; and Israel gave no heed to me. So I let them go after the ways of their own hearts: they will go on in their own ways** (Psalm 81:11-12 LXX). To "heed" means not only to hear the Lord's counsel, or the counsel of godly elders, but to do what they say. Just like the wayward Israelites sought counsel from ungodly sources (Isaiah 29:15 LXX) and followed it instead of God, so does the stubborn woman. Like the Israelites, she seeks self-help from any source but the Bible. **To whom shall I speak, and testify, that he may hearken? behold, thine ears are uncircumcised, and they shall not be able to hear: behold, the word of the Lord is become to them a reproach, they will not at all desire it** (Jeremiah 6:10 LXX).

When a stubborn woman reads a verse about obedience to her husband, she would rather find an excuse to disobey than to humble herself into submission. She will reject God's Word in preference for a theory which is more pleasing to her ears and to her ego. **For the time will come when they will not endure sound doctrine; but after their own lusts shall they heap to themselves teachers, having itching ears; And they shall turn away their ears from the truth, and shall be turned unto fables** (2 Timothy 4:3-4). Further examples of this will be given in Chapter Six.

When the Lord commissioned the saints and prophets to do His will, to speak for Him, and to obey Him with all power, they answered like Moses did, with, **Who am I, that I should go?** (Exodus 3:11 LXX). None of us are anything without the Lord Jesus Christ. When we choose to serve Him, He will circumcise our deaf ears and hard hearts, so that we are able to both hear and obey. Then the blessings will flow. **And it shall come to pass, if thou wilt indeed hear the voice of the Lord thy God, to observe and do all these commands, which I charge thee this day, that the Lord thy God shall set thee on high above all the nations of the earth** (Deuteronomy 28:1 LXX).[15]

When the Bible issues a command, or an ordinance, or a suggestion, or even a hint of a suggestion, the stubborn woman does not ask in humility, Who am I, that I should obey you? Rather, she asks in indignation, Who are you, that I should obey you? This is rebellion. **But it shall come to pass, if thou wilt not hearken to the voice of the Lord thy God, to observe all his commandments, as many as I charge thee this day, then all these curses shall come on thee, and overtake thee** (Deuteronomy 28:15 LXX).[16]

For if any be a hearer of the word, and not a doer, he is like unto a man beholding his natural face in a glass: For he beholdeth himself, and goeth his way, and straightway forgetteth what manner of man he was (James 1:23-24). A stubborn woman might attend church, might hear a good sermon, and might call herself a Christian, but she does not do what the Word of God says. She looks in the mirror and sees herself as a child of God, but walks away and forgets whose daughter she is.

> **Not every one that saith unto me, Lord, Lord, shall enter into the kingdom of heaven; but he that doeth the will of my Father which is in heaven. Many will say to me in that**

---

[15]   For a complete list of blessings, see Deut. 28:1-14 LXX.

[16]   For a complete list of curses, see Deut. 28:15-45 LXX.

day, Lord, Lord, have we not prophesied in thy name? and in thy name have cast out devils? And in thy name done many wonderful works? And then will I profess unto them, I never knew you: depart from me, ye that work iniquity (Matthew 7:21-23).

A stubborn woman who prefers to hear words that are pleasing to her ego has uncircumcised, closed ears. A humble woman softens her ears and listens to the voice God: **He that is of God heareth God's words** (John 8:47).

3) A Stiff Neck.

But they hearkened not, and inclined not their ear, but stiffened their neck more than their fathers did, so as not to hear me, and not to receive correction (Jeremiah 17:23 LXX). A stubborn and stiff-necked woman is proud. She wilfully follows the sinful desires of her own heart. Left unchecked, her heart will eventually cease to feel shame. King Zedekiah

> **did that which was evil in the sight of the Lord his God: he was not ashamed before the prophet [Jeremiah], nor because of the word of the Lord; in that he rebelled against king [Nebuchadnezzar], which he adjured him by God not to do: but he stiffened his neck, and hardened his heart, so as not to return to the Lord God of Israel** (2 Chronicles 36:12-13 LXX).

A stubborn woman goes astray from the path that leads to everlasting life and is too hard-hearted to return to it. She hears the law of the Lord, but casts it "behind her back". **But they turned, and revolted from thee, and cast thy law behind their backs; and they slew thy prophets, who testified against them to turn them back to thee, and they wrought great provocations** (Nehemiah 9:26 LXX).

With the stiff neck of haughtiness and pride, a stubborn woman goes in whatever direction pleases her. She does not bend her knee to God. She lives outside His will, and consequently finds perpetual disappointment and futility. The Lord will leave such a woman to her own devices. **So I let them go after the ways of their own hearts: they will go on in their own ways** (Psalm 81:12 LXX). Choose this day to go in the way of the Lord.

Modern Snapshot
JANET

Janet is a preacher. It all began when she started teaching adult Sunday School in a house church. Undeterred by the Biblical injunction against women teaching Bible doctrine to men, Janet continued because she determined that she taught too well to quit. When a godly friend encouraged her to obey the Word of God in the matter by returning spiritual authority in their home to her husband where it belonged, she listened. For a time, she allowed her husband to take over the study. Unfortunately, she soon deemed his spiritual knowledge inferior to hers. She took this as a sign from God that she was meant to teach. Rejecting her friend's warnings, she obstinately refused to humble herself, and was expelled from the church.

Stubborn in her resolve, she decided to start her own church. Today she is the preacher of that church. John MacArthur[17] would say that church has no preacher, and I would agree with him. If a Bible preacher or godly member of the body of Christ reprove you, and the Word of God substantiates their warning, you need to change your ways. Don't change the Word to suit yourself. Change yourself to suit the Word.

Janet performs all the official functions of a regular pastor. She marries, she baptizes, and she teaches men and women the Word of God. Because her husband defends her and claims that she is justified in his eyes, he takes on a supportive role in the home and in the church. Every Bible verse that prohibits a female from usurping authority over the man, teaching the men, or speaking in church, she calls uninspired. Ironically, the verses

---

[17] According to his website: "John MacArthur is the pastor-teacher of Grace Community Church in Sun Valley, California, as well as an author, speaker, president of The Master's College and Seminary, and featured teacher with the Grace to You ministry". www.gracetoyou.org visited January, 2013

pertaining to a husband's duty to love his wife as his own body are, in her estimation, relevant, vital aspects of Biblical doctrine. She is a hypocrite with a hard heart.

Many people profess to have learned something valuable from Janet. Perhaps she "preaches good". Perhaps the Word of God preaches well no matter who quotes it.

I have a question for you. If the Lord asked you to turn aside from the one thing you thought you loved the most, would you do it? Would you forsake a mother, father, husband, or child for His Name's sake, knowing that you would receive from Jesus a hundredfold and inherit everlasting life in return (Matthew 19:29)? What are you willing to give up for your Redeemer, the One who died for you? If the Lord asks you to give up the authority you've taken from your husband, would He be asking too much?

No doubt Janet's futility and despair are well-hidden behind the walls of her hard heart. She is a stubborn rebel who has blasphemed the Word of God by wilfully disobeying Him. It is not yet too late for Janet to change her ways. Neither is it too late for you.

To day if ye will hear his voice, harden not your hearts (Hebrews 4:7b).

Summary

A hard-hearted woman is stubborn and obstinate. She has a stiff neck and is uncircumcised in her heart and ears. She fails to fear, know, understand, or obey the Lord Jesus Christ. Instead of walking in His ways, she walks in her own. When circumstances reveal to her the error of her ways, she refuses instruction and turns her back on good counsel. She is impenitent and unashamed. **A stubborn servant will not be reproved by words: for even if he understands, still he will not obey** (Proverbs 29:19 LXX).

Who Shall Deliver Me?

And be not as your fathers, and your brethren, who revolted from the Lord God of their fathers, and he gave them up to desolation, as ye

see. And now harden not your hearts, as your fathers did: give glory to the Lord God, and enter into his sanctuary, which he has sanctified for ever: and serve the Lord your God, and he shall turn away his fierce anger from you (2 Chronicles 30:7-8 LXX).

- And this I pray, that your love may abound yet more and more in knowledge and in all judgment; That ye may approve things that are excellent; that ye may be sincere and without offence till the day of Christ; Being filled with the fruits of righteousness, which are by Jesus Christ, unto the glory and praise of God (Philippians 1:9-11).
- For it is God which worketh in you both to will and to do of his good pleasure (Philippians 2:13).
- Fear not, little flock; for it is your Father's good pleasure to give you the kingdom (Luke 12:32).

How Can I Be Obedient?

1. Soften your heart (Romans 2:29).
2. Open your ears (John 8:47).
3. Loosen your stiff neck (Deut. 10:16 LXX).
4. Read the Word (Psalm 119:105 LXX).
5. Memorize the Word (Romans 2:15).
6. Do what it says (James 1:23).
7. Thank the Lord for blessing you (1 Cor. 15:57).

Think on These Things

1. *Is my heart soft towards my husband?*
   1 Peter 3:1

2. *Do I show my children the joy of the Lord?*
   Col. 3:16

3. *Do I praise God for all His gifts?*
   1 Peter 4:11

4. *Am I content with what God has given me?*
   Heb. 13:5
5. *Do I listen only to things that are virtuous?*
   James 1:25
6. *Am I consistent in my walk with the Lord?*
   1 John 1:6
7. *Am I teachable, flexible, and eager to learn more of God?*
   Titus 2:4
8. *How do I respond to the love and kindness of my Saviour?*
   Titus 3:4-7
9. *How can my life show humility?*
   Phil. 2:3-4
10. *How can I keep my heart pure?*
    1 Peter 1:22, Heb. 10:22

CHAPTER THREE

A STRIFE AMONG THEM

LUKE 22:24

Profile #3: The Clamorous Woman

Let All . . . Clamour . . . Be Put Away From You (Ephesians 4:31)

MARTHA

We meet Martha, the sister of Mary, in Luke 10:38. She was serving Jesus and the disciples at her home in Bethany. On this occasion, when Jesus was present, Mary sat at His feet and listened to His words, **But Martha was cumbered about much serving, and came to him, and said, Lord, dost thou not care that my sister hath left me to serve alone? bid her therefore that she help me** (Luke 10:40).

Martha saw her serving responsibilities as a burden, not a blessing. She envied Mary's choice to sit at Jesus' feet and sought to deprive her of it. She approached Jesus to complain and accused Him of not noticing or caring about her hard work relative to her sister's. She demanded that He intervene on her behalf. Martha displayed a lack of respect, restraint, and charity.

The story continues. **And Jesus answered and said unto her, Martha, Martha, thou art careful and troubled about many things: But one thing is needful: and Mary hath chosen that good part, which shall not be taken away from her** (Luke 10:41-42). In these passages, Jesus identified Martha's problem, offered her a solution, admonished her, and provided her with a positive example to learn from. I do not think that

Martha expected Mary to receive Jesus' praise when it was clear from her request that her desire was to see Mary reprimanded. Did she have ears to hear?

Fast forward to the death of Lazarus, as told in John 11:

> **Then Martha, as soon as she heard that Jesus was coming, went and met him: but Mary sat still in the house. Then said Martha unto Jesus, Lord, if thou hadst been here, my brother had not died. But I know, that even now, whatsoever thou wilt ask of God, God will give it thee. Jesus saith unto her, Thy brother shall rise again. Martha saith unto him, I know that he shall rise again in the resurrection at the last day. Jesus said unto her, I am the resurrection, and the life: he that believeth in me, though he were dead, yet shall he live: And whosoever liveth and believeth in me shall never die. Believest thou this? She saith unto him, Yea, Lord: I believe that thou art the Christ, the Son of God, which should come into the world. And when she had so said, she went her way, and called Mary her sister secretly, saying, The Master is come, and calleth for thee. As soon as she heard that, she arose quickly, and came unto him** (John 11:20-29).

Martha's ears were open, but still, they did not hear. Again, she approached Jesus to accuse and complain. She debated. She contended, she devised, and she strove. She was clamorous.

How Does a Woman Display Clamour?

Let all bitterness, and wrath, and anger, and clamour, and evil speaking, be put away from you, with all malice (Ephesians 4:31). Clamour is a protest or a demand. It is a confused noise.[1] When a person is clamorous, there is no peace or order. There is confusion, unrest, chaos, and disobedience. **For God is not the author of confusion, but of peace, as in all the churches of the saints** (1 Corinthians 14:33). In the church,

---

[1]   Oxford Reference Dictionary

Paige Coleman

such behaviour is divisive and destructive. Clamour, bitterness, wrath, anger, and evil speaking cause division. They work against the Spirit of God by destroying the unity of the church. This is why we must put them away from us.[2]

Clamour, by definition, involves speech. A clamorous woman, therefore, tends to be loud and outspoken. As a divisive member of the church, her tongue **defileth the whole body, and setteth on fire the courses of nature; and it is set on fire of hell** (James 3:6b). Women, proficient communicators, are not solely responsible for spreading division in the church. However, they can be very good at it!

Division within the church is incited or condoned when clamour is not only tolerated within our hearts and minds, but is let loose from our tongues in an unrestrained display of vanity and self-will. A mouth that speaks in such ways **is an unruly evil, full of deadly poison** (James 3:8b).

The following qualifiers describe the manner of speech a clamorous woman habituates: 1) she strives, 2) she accuses, 3) she debates, and 4) she is seditious.

1) She strives.

And the servant of the Lord must not strive; but be gentle unto all men, apt to teach, patient (2 Timothy 2:24). To strive is to rigorously exert oneself. The related word, "strife," is the tumult that characterizes such rigorous exertions. There are two kinds of striving discussed in the Bible. One is to exert God's will in a committed and self-sacrificial manner for God's glory. For example, in Luke 13:24, we are told how to strive personally: **Strive to enter in at the strait gate** and in Philippians 1:27, we are told how to strive as a church: **with one mind striving together for the faith of the gospel.** These are positive Biblical examples of striving. The other way to strive is to exert your own will in a committed and selfish manner for your own glory: **Let nothing be done through strife or vainglory; but in lowliness of mind let each esteem other better than themselves** (Philippians 2:3).

---

[2]   1 Corinthians 5:13, Ephesians 4:25, 2 Timothy 3:5.

46

Strife is also defined as conflict or struggle. A woman who acts in strife takes an oppositional stance on a matter and then struggles to prove herself correct. **Of these things put them in remembrance, charging them before the Lord that they strive not about words to no profit** (2 Timothy 2:14). Such striving is unfruitful and unedifying. **Let no corrupt communication proceed out of your mouth, but that which is good to the use of edifying, that it may minister grace unto the hearers** (Ephesians 4:29). If a discussion must arise about a matter of doctrine, the striving woman's need to be correct supersedes her need to impart the truth. A contentious argumentative woman, therefore, strives not for godliness in God's eyes, but for self-righteousness, which is godliness in the eyes of others for the sake of her own reputation and glory.

Because conflict is associated with the striving woman, it is difficult for her to find contentment, sobriety, or peace. She is characterized by tension and angst, or anxiety. As a result, she is prone to sleeplessness, distress, or illness. She is a perfectionist who fusses over the little things. The Bible warns us against taking on such worry: **Be careful for nothing; but in every thing by prayer and supplication with thanksgiving let your requests be made known unto God. And the peace of God, which passeth all understanding, shall keep your hearts and minds through Christ Jesus** (Philippians 4:6-7). Instead of resting in the peace and confidence of Christ, the clamorous woman frets. She dramatizes the mundane and exaggerates for effect, causing mistruths and miscommunication to come out of her mouth. **But as he which hath called you is holy, so be ye holy in all manner of conversation** (1 Peter 1:15). Although she may be just as saved by the blood of Christ as you are, she has formed habits that require a great deal of soul-wrenching to break.

For where envying and strife is, there is confusion and every evil work (James 3:16). A striving woman feels competitive against others, speaking in anger, backstabbing, and causing tumults. **Anger slays even wise men; yet a submissive answer turns away wrath: but a grievous word stirs up anger** (Proverbs 15:1 LXX). She lacks meekness, meaning that she is easily offended. She reacts defensively and proudly, often assuming that she is under attack when she is not. As a result, the people around her tread lightly lest they upset her.

Jesus, our perfect example, was surrounded by the sullied hearts of lost sinners and had every reason to be offended by them, but He chose not to be. His inestimable grace was revealed not only in the way He patiently and lovingly tolerated their presence, but also in that He suffered and died for them to render their hearts pure before God. Although He seemed to have the greatest weight to bear, yet His peaceful, meek manner is the lightest burden of all. **Take my yoke upon you, and learn of me; for I am meek and lowly in heart: and ye shall find rest unto your souls** (Matthew 11:29).

A striving woman is not focused in singleness of mind on the things of Christ. She allows herself to be derailed and distracted. **With much wood fire increases; but where there is not a double-minded man, strife ceases** (Proverbs 26:20 LXX). Instead of focusing on the fulfillment of God's will in her life, she picks up the cares of this world and allows them to throw her off the path of righteousness. **Has it not been told thee, O man, what is good? or what does the Lord require of thee, but to do justice, and love mercy, and be ready to walk with the Lord thy God?** (Micah 6:8 LXX). To walk with God in the Spirit is to cultivate a rested, peaceful soul.

Then Martha, as soon as she heard that Jesus was coming, went and met him: but Mary sat still in the house (John 11:20). Martha was so anxious to confront Jesus that she would not sit still and wait for His arrival. Contrary to her sister, Mary, who **sat still**, Martha strove. Just as she was anxious to complain to Jesus about Mary in Luke 10:40, here she was intent once again on her purpose, which was to give the Holy One of Israel a piece of her mind.

2) She accuses.

God will punish the unjust, **but chiefly them that walk after the flesh in the lust of uncleanness, and despise government. Presumptuous are they, selfwilled, they are not afraid to speak evil of dignities. Whereas angels, which are greater in power and might, bring not railing accusation against them before the Lord** (2 Peter 2:10-11). "Dignities" are "dignitaries", those who hold a position of authority in the world or the church. They include kings, preachers, angels, police officers, and elders, among others. Your husband is a dignitary. He is your spiritual head; he outranks you (1 Corinthians 11:3). If you think your husband deserves an accusatory remark from time to time, then you are speaking evil of a dignitary, and you err.

Satan also holds rank as a dignitary, but he does not have authority over you.[3] If you are saved, you belong to Christ and have His protection. We are told, **Resist the devil, and he will flee from you** (James 4:7b). We all know that the devil deserves a word or two of open rebuke, but it is not our place to give it.

In Jude 1:8, we are warned to never speak evil of dignities. The next verse gives us an example. **Yet Michael the archangel, when contending with the devil he disputed about the body of Moses, durst not bring against him a railing accusation, but said, The Lord rebuke thee** (Jude 1:9). The Lord will rebuke those who outrank us in the manner and hour that He chooses. No matter how justified we may feel to do so ourselves, we must resist. A clamorous woman does not resist.

The clamorous woman does not wait on the Lord in faith to correct those who outrank her. She speaks from the estimation of her own authority, without stopping to consider God's. She is **presumptuous** and **selfwilled** (1 Peter 2:10b). She is not afraid to speak offensively of others. She fails to put her faith ahead of her tongue, and she, along with the Pharisees that came before her, will **speak evil of those things which they know not** (Jude 1:10a).

God will deliver justice where it is due. In Numbers 12, Miriam and Aaron spoke evil of Moses because he married an Ethiopian woman. They esteemed themselves higher than they ought to, saying, **Has the Lord spoken to Moses only? has he not also spoken to us? and the Lord heard it** (Numbers 12:2 LXX). Moses, being so meek that he felt no offense against them for their accusation, consequently gave God every reason to rebuke them on his behalf. God brought the three of them together and said to Miriam and Aaron, **And why were ye not afraid to speak against my servant Moses? And the great anger of the Lord was upon them** (Numbers 12:8b, 9a LXX).

---

[3]   Psalm 8:5 LX, John 12:31, Jude 9

Miriam was struck with leprosy. Even though Aaron claimed that they sinned in ignorance, and cried out to the Lord on Miriam's behalf, it was only after Moses begged the Lord to heal her that God responded, saying, **If her father had only spit in her face, would she not be ashamed seven days? let her be set apart seven days without the camp, and afterwards she shall come in** (Numbers 12:14 LXX).

Miriam was clamorous, and was punished for it. She spoke against Moses. Whether he was her brother or not, he was a dignitary in God's eyes, and he outranked her. She may have thought that she had a valid point against him, but it was not her place to say so. God will justify, condemn, or pardon whom He will; He is the Avenger of all evil, not us. **Dearly beloved, avenge not yourselves, but rather give place unto wrath: for it is written, Vengeance is mine; I will repay, saith the Lord** (Romans 12:19).

Shortly after I was married, I met a meek, Christian woman who was rather homely in appearance. Still in the habit of judging others according to worldly standards, I behaved somewhat disdainfully toward her and commented on her appearance to my husband. A few years later, I saw her again. I had changed; she had not. Although she looked and acted the same, I did not see drab. I did not see anything unattractive. I saw a beautiful, feminine Christian woman with a heart for Christ. All the words that came out of her mouth were Biblical, edifying, and *wise*. Out of sincere respect for her, and a desire to be more like her, I befriended her. The privilege was mine; the glory was God's. That meek, unfashionable girl was a gem, awarded low regard by men, but given priceless worth by her Father in heaven.

A clamorous woman speaks in ignorance against her sisters in Christ. **Let the deceitful lips become dumb, which speak iniquity against the righteous with pride and scorn** (Psalm 31:18 LXX). In Titus 2, we see that women are pointedly reminded to refrain from making false accusations: **The aged women likewise, that they be in behaviour as becometh holiness, not false accusers, not given to much wine, teachers of good things** (Titus 2:3).

What we say is of the utmost importance. Our ability to control our speech contributes to our ability to control our entire bodies. **If any man offend not in word, the same is a perfect man, and able also to**

bridle the whole body (James 3:2b). Please learn to control your tongue. **Therewith bless we God, even the Father; and therewith curse we men, which are made after the similitude of God. Out of the same mouth proceedeth blessing and cursing. My brethren, these things ought not so to be** (James 3:9-10).

Then said Martha unto Jesus, Lord, if thou hadst been here, my brother had not died (John 11:21). The first words out of Martha's mouth to the Son of God were accusatory. Martha spoke without understanding against Jesus Christ. He wasn't just any dignitary—He was *the* dignitary— the Son of God. There is one called **the accuser of our brethren . . . which accused them before our God day and night** (Revelation 12:10b). He is **that old serpent, called the Devil, and Satan, which deceiveth the whole world** (Revelation 12:9a). Please don't do his job for him.

3) She debates.

A clamorous woman resists peaceable conversation. She always has a word to say and an opinion to assert. The subject matter is inconsequential to her need to talk; she will debate any subject in an attempt to appear knowledgeable. A debate is by definition oppositional. The motivation of a clamorous woman is therefore steeped in contrariness. She will contest and refute the views of her opponents in order to gain a perceived advantage, lengthening a discussion into an unedifying and inharmonious debacle. Words that sow such discord are corrupt; they are errant "evil-speakings". **Wherefore laying aside all malice, and all guile, and hypocrisies and envies, and all evil speakings, As newborn babes, desire the sincere milk of the word, that ye may grow thereby: If so be ye have tasted that the Lord is gracious** (1 Peter 2:1-3).

The more you fill up your heart and mind with the Word of God, the more you will grow in the Spirit and the less you will be inclined to debate, to strive, or to be contentious. If what you want to say will not edify or admonish the listener in Christ, *do not say it.*

In the church, matters of doctrine, legalism and "grey areas" are commonly debated and contested. Paul warns Timothy about this very thing:

> **If any man . . . consent not to wholesome words, even the words of our Lord Jesus Christ, and to the doctrine which is according to godliness; He is proud, knowing nothing, but doting about questions and strifes of words, whereof cometh envy, strife, railings, evil surmisings, Perverse disputings of men of corrupt minds, and destitute of the truth, supposing that gain is godliness: from such withdraw thyself** (1 Timothy 6:3-5).

Chasing down strifes of words is like trying to walk a straight path while constantly getting distracted by what lies in the ditch alongside it. The deeper a matter is contested, the deeper into the ditch a woman goes. Soon, she can no longer see the sun or the path from which she came. If a woman departs from the Word of God in order to debate or defend an opinion, she is in danger of spreading false doctrine. She is clamorous and to be avoided.

When her words become excessive as well as contrary, the contentious woman who utters them is called a "nag". The Bible also refers to this as railing. Like the incessant dripping of rain will **drive a man out of his house; so also does a railing woman drive a man out of his own house** (Proverbs 27:15 LXX). The presence of a railing woman can become insufferable. **It is better to dwell on the corner of a roof, than with a railing woman in an open house** (Proverbs 25:24 LXX). A clamorous, debating, railing woman feels the need to have the last word.

The dialogue of Martha and Jesus recorded in John 11:21-28 is condensed as follows. Martha had just finished telling Jesus that Lazarus was dead because Jesus hadn't arrived on time.

Martha: **I know, that even now, whatsoever thou wilt ask of God, God will give it thee.**
Jesus: **Thy brother shall rise again.**
Martha: **I know that he shall rise again in the resurrection at the last day.**
Jesus: **I am the resurrection, and the life: he that believeth in me, though he were dead, yet shall he live: And whosoever liveth and believeth in me shall never die. Believest thou this?**

Martha: **Yea, Lord: I believe that thou art the Christ, the Son of God, which should come into the world** (John 11:21-27).

Martha was using the pious words of a religious woman but she did not understand Jesus' will or intention. Twice, she asserts, "I know", but she did not know that Jesus was talking about resurrecting Lazarus from the dead that very day. She was too busy talking her faith to actually feel her faith. As a result, she could not *hear* what Jesus was trying to tell her. **And when she had so said, she went her way** (John 11:21-28a). After having the last word, she walked away—from Jesus Christ.

Martha's words spoken after arriving at the cave where Lazarus was buried further reveal her contention. She followed Jesus there and heard Him bid the stone be removed. Her heart did not leap in faith for joy at the implications of what Jesus was saying. Instead, she revealed the state of her heart by offering another verbal protest. She said, **Lord, by this time he stinketh: for he hath been dead four days** (John 11:39b). Despite her earlier claim of faith, Martha had no idea what was about to happen. Once again, Jesus offered her correction. **Jesus saith unto her, Said I not unto thee, that, if thou wouldest believe, thou shouldest see the glory of God?** (John 11:40a). Believe on the Lord Jesus Christ. Listen when He speaks and *hear* His Words. **Wherefore, my beloved brethren, let every man be swift to hear, slow to speak, slow to wrath** (James 1:19).

4) She is seditious.

To be seditious is to incite rebellion or discontentment against an established authority. In Galatians 5:20, Paul identifies sedition as a work of the flesh. He tells us that **the works of the flesh are manifest** (Galatians 5:19) in those whose inner battle between the flesh and spirit has been lost to the flesh. In the church, these battles cause division.

Paul experienced this divisiveness in the Corinthian church as well and describes his disappointment: **For I fear, lest, when I come, I shall not find you such as I would, and that I shall be found unto you such as ye would not: lest there be debates, envyings, wraths, strifes, backbitings, whisperings, swellings, tumults** (2 Corinthians 12:20). A clamorous woman is seditious; she promotes discord and rebellion with her words.

High school is not yet far enough in my past for me to forget how some girls railed against one another at every opportunity. Whether those opportunities were actual or contrived, the occurrence invariably caused a delirium of blood-lust to unleash between them. They were fascinated by their ability to incite a fight by using provocative words. **Thou hatest, O Lord, all them that work iniquity** (Psalm 5:5 LXX). I vividly recall the iniquitous relish in one girl's eyes as she informed another of all the horrible things she had heard her "best friend" say about her behind her back. Soon, there she was, brawling with this girl outside the office doors, railing at her with her fists. **But shun profane and vain babblings: for they will increase unto more ungodliness** (2 Timothy 2:16).

Regrettably, today's church is not so different. A monstrously shameful occurrence is this very same behaviour enacted by brothers and sisters in Christ—believers provoking believers, resorting to petty gossiping, seedy recriminations, high-mindedness, and false humility. Paul said, **For I fear . . . I shall bewail many which have sinned already, and have not repented** (2 Corinthians 12:20a, 21). Such seditious behaviour was practised by the scribes and Pharisees against Jesus, who **began to urge him vehemently, and to provoke him to speak of many things: Laying wait for him, and seeking to catch something out of his mouth, that they might accuse him** (Luke 11: 53-54).

With God as our undisputed, sovereign authority, there is no question that to stir up strife among the brethren is sedition. Because it works against the unity of the body of Christ, it thwarts the effectiveness of the church, rendering it unfruitful, and giving all its members, including its Head, a bad name. For this reason, we are encouraged to **Be kindly affectioned one to another with brotherly love; in honour preferring one another** (Romans 12:10).

Peter exhorts us: **Finally, be ye all of one mind, having compassion one of another, love as brethren, be pitiful, be courteous: not rendering evil for evil, or railing for railing: but contrariwise blessing; knowing that ye are thereunto called, that ye should inherit a blessing** (1 Peter 3:8-9). As members of the body of Christ, it is our privilege to build one another up in love. This is a blessing. God has gifted us for this purpose.

We are not to use words to incite rebellion and strife, contention and tumults; we are to **speak every man truth with his neighbour: for we are members one of another** (Ephesians 4:25).

How did Martha use her words? As soon as Martha returned from having run out to meet Jesus (John 11:28), she **called Mary her sister secretly, saying, The Master is come, and calleth for thee. As soon as [Mary] heard that, she arose quickly, and came unto him . . . . Then when Mary was come where Jesus was, and saw him, she fell down at his feet, saying unto him, Lord, if thou hadst been here, my brother had not died** (John 11:28-29, 32). The words that came out of Mary's mouth when she met Jesus were the exact same words that had come out of Martha's mouth earlier (John 11:21). Had Martha bemoaned Jesus' failure to arrive on time to Mary earlier, effectively speaking in seditious terms and planting the seed of doubt in Mary's mind? I think that she did.

The fact that Martha **secretly** told Mary that Jesus asked for her suggests deceit. There is no indication in the text that Mary had actually been summoned by Jesus. It seems that Martha complained to Jesus to no avail, so she sent Mary to finish the task for her. Note how Jesus responded in the very next verse: **When Jesus therefore saw [Mary] weeping, and the Jews also weeping which came with her, he groaned in the spirit, and was troubled** (John 11:33). What do you think troubled Him so?

Martha's actions were seditious. She caused undue disbelief and grief to infect her household, which was a **household of faith** (Galatians 6:10b). Nevertheless, John 11:5 assures us that **Jesus loved Martha, and her sister, and Lazarus.** Jesus loves all the saints. Our mistakes can always be brought before His feet in sorrow and repentance, with the confidence that God will grant us the correction that we need and the forgiveness that we ask for (1 John 1:9).

Jesus would have us all

> **know the love of Christ, which passeth knowledge, that ye might be filled with all the fullness of God. Now unto him that is able to do exceeding abundantly above all that we ask or think, according to the power that worketh in us, Unto him be glory in the church by Christ Jesus throughout all ages, world without end. Amen.** (Ephesians 3:19-21).

Modern Snapshot
GWEN

Gwen grew up in a Christian home and strove to accomplish all that was expected of her. In church, she was moral and helpful. At home, she was studious and meticulous. Her willingness to work won her the favour of most church members, and she was recognized as a highly capable, dependable young adult. However, unbeknownst to those who knew her at church, she commonly experienced great inner turmoil. The pressures that she placed upon herself to appear righteous and capable on the outside caused her much consternation and anxiety on the inside. Inwardly, she felt embittered by the success of others because their success diminished her own. As a result, she was envious and competitive.

Although highly intelligent, she constantly strove to prove it. She was defensive and uptight. When her opinion was neither heeded nor given the appropriate amount of reverence, she was offended and confused. Instead of gracefully removing herself from a debate, she would strive all the more rigorously to win a futile point.

When Gwen attended university, she became so besotted with worldly wisdom that pride and condescension characterized her speech. Soon she equated domestic work with slavery and oppression because academia merited more "respect". After she and her existentialist boyfriend became physically intimate, her shame provoked her to deny God. Growing further disillusioned by the hypocritical conduct of fellow nominal Christians, she decided that the Bible was irrelevant and stated that she was no longer a Christian. From this point on, she strove to find the meaning of "good" apart from God.

Today, Gwen mocks Christians. She disdains their diminutive intellectual status and takes it upon herself to coerce them into abandoning their "primitive" faith. She has much in common with nominal Christians, but despises Bible-believing men and women of integrity. At every opportunity, she will back-bite, scorn, slander, and rail against them. She lies and slanders to elicit rifts between them. She falsely accuses their **good conversation in Christ** (1 Peter 3:16b).

While all these things occur, Gwen retains her reputation as a clever, hard-working young woman. Few suspect that her beautiful, spotless exterior hides a tumultuous and unclean heart.

Let all bitterness, and wrath, and anger, and clamour, and evil speaking, be put away from you, with all malice (Ephesians 4:31).

Summary

Clamorous women strive; they are driven to accomplish tasks that develop from the desire for vain glory. They accuse; indiscriminately, they esteem themselves higher than those around them and take it upon themselves to offer "correction". They debate; they defensively attempt to prove themselves most righteous and their opinions most reliable. They are motivated by pride and envy. Clamorous women are seditious; they provoke discontentment and disunity in the church, rebelling against God's will and His authority.

One definition of clamour is "a loud and persistent noise". With her mouth, a clamorous woman disrupts the peace by railing and backbiting. We are told, **Open thy mouth with the word of God, and judge all fairly** (Proverbs 31:8 LXX). The virtuous Proverbs 31 woman **opens her mouth heedfully and with propriety, and controls her tongue** (Proverbs 31:24 LXX). It matters what comes out of our mouths. It is a clear reflection of what abides in our hearts.

Who Shall Deliver Me?

And Enoch also, the seventh from Adam, prophesied of these, saying, behold, the Lord cometh with ten thousands of his saints, To execute judgment upon all, and to convince all that are ungodly among them of all their ungodly deeds which they have ungodly committed, and of all their hard speeches which ungodly sinners have spoken against him. These are murmurers, complainers, walking after their own lusts; and their mouth speaketh great swelling words, having men's persons in admiration because of advantage. But, beloved, remember ye the words which were spoken before of the apostles of

our Lord Jesus Christ; How that they told you there would be mockers in the last time, who should walk after their own ungodly lusts. These be they who separate themselves, sensual, having not the Spirit.

But ye, beloved, building up yourselves on your most holy faith, praying in the Holy Ghost, Keep yourselves in the love of God, looking for the mercy of our Lord Jesus Christ unto eternal life. And of some have compassion, making a difference: And others save with fear, pulling them out of the fire; hating even the garment spotted by the flesh.

Now unto him that is able to keep you from falling, and to present you faultless before the presence of his glory with exceeding joy, To the only wise God our Saviour, be glory and majesty, dominion and power, both now and ever. Amen (Jude 14-25).

- But whoso keepeth his word, in him verily is the love of God perfected: hereby know we that we are in him (1 John 2:5).
- Seek ye the Lord, and when ye find him, call upon him; and when he shall draw nigh to you, let the ungodly leave his ways, and the transgressor his counsels: and let him return to the Lord, and he shall find mercy; for he shall abundantly pardon your sins (Isaiah 55:6-7 LXX).
- Let us therefore come boldly unto the throne of grace, that we may obtain mercy, and find grace to help in time of need (Hebrews 4:16).
- Sacrifice to God is a broken spirit: a broken and humbled heart God will not despise (Psalm 51:17 LXX).

How Can I Be Peaceable?

1. Humble yourself (1 Peter 5:5).
2. Esteem others higher than yourself (Philippians 2:3).
3. Avoid foolish and argumentative questions (2 Timothy 2:23).
4. Shun contention (2 Timothy 2:16).
5. Edify with your words (1 Thessalonians 5:11).
6. Be careful for nothing (Philippians 4:6).
7. Live peaceably (Hebrews 12:14).

Think on These Things

1. Am I gentle in my dealings with others?
    2 Timothy 2:24
2. Do I spend time alone with God, thinking of things that are lovely and true?
    Col. 3:1,2
3. Do I allow Christ to work in me rather than relying on myself?
    Heb. 13:20-21
4. Am I steadfast in my faith in God?
    James 1:5-6
5. How do I keep from doing wrong?
    James 4:7
6. Do I honour God with my words?
    Eph. 4:29
7. How do I deal with complaints and rebellion?
    1 Pet. 3:8-9
8. How can I know the right words?
    1 Thes. 4:6
9. How can I prevent bitterness?
    Col. 3:13-14
10. How can I control my tongue?
    1 John 2:10
11. Why should I not condemn others?
    Rom. 14:4, Mat. 7:2, 1 Cor. 4:5
12. How can I keep my priorities straight?
    Mat. 6:33, 1 Cor. 11:28

CHAPTER FOUR

A VESSEL FULL OF HOLES
PROVERBS 23:27 LXX

STUDY BREAK
Cheating on God

B ecause our relationship to God is illustrated Biblically in the same way that the covenant of marriage is, when His people are disloyal to Him, they are described in adulterous terms. The terms "adulterer", "adulteress", "idolater", "fornicator", "whore", "harlot, and "strange woman" are used synonymously in this way. However, not all people or nations were originally God-fearing. Those that at one time belonged to God but later turned away "commit adultery" because they violated their "marriage" contract with God (Hosea 4:14 LXX).[1] King David describes this as having **dealt unrighteously in [God's] covenant** (Psalm 44:17 LXX). Those that were never "married" to God are called "fornicators" (Hosea 4:14 LXX) because they are "lovers" of many gods (Ezekiel 23:5 LXX), not having been loyal to any particular one.

When the Bible describes the unfaithful "harlot" or "whore", she is female, but not necessary a single person. She is also a nation. For example, the "harlot" of Jeremiah 3 and Ezekiel 16 is Jerusalem; the adulteress Hosea married represents the Israelites, as do the sisters Aholah and Aholibah of Ezekiel 23. The "harlot" of Nahum 3 is Nineveh. The "harlot" of Isaiah 23

---

[1]   Please note that getting married to a man on this earth is not an act of adultery against God, as some false teachers claim.

is Tyre. Then there is the "great whore" of Babylon in Revelation 17. These are a just a few Old Testament examples which prove that this marital parallel also speaks of the nations of the world. In other words, an entire nation can **go a-whoring after the strange gods** (Deuteronomy 31:16b LXX).

In the New Testament (and in Old Testament prophecies), the church is likened to a bride whose marital home is being prepared for her in heaven (John 14:2). In keeping with Jewish wedding tradition, the return of the bridegroom to collect His bride is unpredictable and sudden.[2] While she is waiting for Him, she is to remain faithful (Matthew 25:4). She must understand that time in her temporary home is to be used productively in service to her Lord (Matthew 25:27). When the bridegroom (the Lord) returns, there will be a reckoning—a time when the bride is to give answer for her faithfulness to him, or lack thereof (Matthew 25:19). How is this faithfulness ensured? It begins with our thoughts.

James 3 describes two types of wisdom: that which comes from above (James 3:17) and that which comes from below (James 3:15). The first is godly wisdom. It is sought by believers who trust in God for fulfillment. The latter is devilish wisdom. It is sought by unbelievers who look to the world for fulfillment. Those who seek godly wisdom and instruction are His faithful bride. She is intellectually loyal to Him.

When believers ascribe to worldly wisdom, seeking advice or counsel from humanist philosophy or occult magic, they have removed their loyalty from Biblical wisdom and given it to earthly wisdom. **They asked counsel by means of signs, and they reported answer to them by their staves: they have gone astray in a spirit of whoredom, and gone grievously a-whoring from their God** (Hosea 4:12 LXX). A "spirit of whoredom" is the desire to seek knowledge and counsel from the world (Satan) and not from heaven (God).

Satan, as the **god of this world hath blinded the minds of them which believe not** (2 Corinthians 4:4). He is the ultimate provider of earthly wisdom. He is the father of lies (John 8:44). He spreads false doctrines and false religions to ensnare God's people, using **great swelling words of vanity** (2 Peter 2:18).

---

2   Matthew 25:13, 1 Thessalonians 5:2

Satanic wisdom is by definition "sensual" (James 3:15). This means "of the flesh" (Romans 9:8a), carnal (Romans 8:7a), and lustful (James 1:14). Satanic wisdom itches people's ears (2 Timothy 4:3). It flatters them and appeals to their ego. In **fulfilling the desires of the flesh and of the mind** (Ephesians 2:3), they hear, contemplate, harbour, and believe vain philosophies and the traditions of men (Colossians 2:8). This is an act of war against the soul (1 Peter 2:11). God says, **Woe to them that deepen their counsel, and not by the Lord** (Isaiah 29:15a LXX).

Many of us have heard the startling statistics which show that 75% of "Christian" students lose their faith in their first year of college or university. This is because they have been beguiled by worldly wisdom. Vain philosophies (Colossians 2:8) have ensnared them and they have become "puffed up" on worldly knowledge (1 Corinthians 8:1). They have proven themselves unfaithful by **trusting in wickedness** (Isaiah 47:10a LXX) and will therefore **have no deliverance** (Isaiah 47:15b LXX). Instead of trusting in the God of the Bible,[3] they have trusted in vanities.

Satan is the adversary (1 Peter 5:8). Imagine giving away your loyalty to the enemy of your "bridegroom" while He is away. This is why God's jealousy, wrath, and vengeance are kindled into an unquenchable fire against those who seek worldly wisdom: **And I will be avenged on thee with the vengeance of an adulteress, and I will bring upon thee blood of fury and jealousy** (Ezekiel 16:38 LXX).

Paul wrote to the Corinthians, **For I am jealous over you with a godly jealousy: for I have espoused you to one husband, that I may present you as a chaste virgin to Christ** (2 Corinthians 11:2). To be espoused to one husband is to seek and find fulfillment in Him alone. Wisdom is sought and received by His Word alone. An unsullied believer has remained faithful to His Word and to His Way. She is a chaste virgin because she is **unspotted from the world** (James 1:27b).

---

3   Ezekiel 23:43 LXX, Hosea 3:1 LXX, 1 Corinthians 6:15-16, 2 Corinthians 11:2

The Strange Woman

We are told that the strange woman's **house is the way of hell, leading down to the chambers of death** (Proverbs 7:27 LXX).[4] Proverbs 2:18 LXX says that **she has fixed her house near death, and guided her wheels near Hades with the giants.** She has **wounded and cast down many, and those whom she has slain are innumerable** (Proverbs 7:25 LXX). She looks out of the window of her house in search of a potential victim (Proverbs 7:6 LXX). Does this sound like the treacherous actions of a single woman? No, because the **strange and wicked woman** (Proverbs 7:4 LXX) is more than just a seductive fornicator. She represents the devil and her "house" is the world.

The word "strange" in the Bible is used to indicate that which is not of God. God describes strangers as those who are alienated from His soul (Ezekiel 23:18 LXX). "Strange gods"[5], "strange children"[6] and "strange women"[7] are those who have "turned aside"[8] from the Lord and cause others to do the same. Nehemiah wrote

> **Did not Solomon king of Israel sin thus? though there was no king like him among many nations, and he was beloved of God, and God made him king over all Israel; yet strange women turned him aside. So we will not hearken to you to do all this evil, to break covenant with our God,—to marry strange wives** (Nehemiah 13:26-27 LXX).

---

[4] Brothels were idol-worshipping and incense burning cesspools, having a god available for every man of every nation to pay homage to. In Numbers 25, for example, when the Israelites went "a-whoring" after the daughters of Moab, the girls "called them to the sacrifices of their idols; and the people ate of their sacrifices, and worshipped their idols. And Israel consecrated themselves to Beelphegor; and the Lord was very angry with Israel" vs. 2-3 LXX.

[5] Genesis 35:2,4, Deuteronomy 32:12, 16, Joshua 24:20, 23, Judges 10:16, I Samuel 7:3, 2 Chronicles 33:15, Psalm 44:20, 81:9, Isaiah 43:12, Jeremiah 5:19, Daniel 11:39, Malachi 2:11

[6] Psalm 144:7,11, Hosea 5:7

[7] 1 Kings 11:1, Nehemiah 13:26, Proverbs 2:16, 5:3, 20, 6:24, 7:5, 23:27, 33

[8] Deuteronomy 31:29, Joshua 23:6, 12-13, Psalm 44:18, 125:5, Proverbs 4:27, 7:25, Isaiah 29:21, 30:11, Ezekiel 14:5, Lamentations 3:35, Daniel 9:5, Hosea 7:16, Malachi 2:8

In Proverbs 7:25 LXX, Solomon says to his son, **Let not thine heart turn aside to her ways**. Her ways are the devices of Satan.

1 John 5:19b says that the **whole world lieth in wickedness.** Paul said we live **in the midst of a crooked and perverse nation** (Philippians 2:15b). John tells us to **Love not the world, neither the things that are in the world** (1 John 2:15a). James says that those who love the world are the enemies of God (James 4:4).

Satan is the **god of this world** (2 Corinthians 4:4). He is **the tempter** (Matthew 4:3a). He is the purveyor of influence; he is the **prince of the power of the air, the spirit that now worketh in the children of disobedience** (Ephesians 2:2). He is responsible for **spiritual wickedness in high places** (Ephesians 6:12). It is here, in this world, that **every high thing that exalteth itself against the knowledge of God** (2 Corinthians 10:5) is a satanic strong hold. The things that are in the world are never to be consumed by the children of righteousness, the children of God. **For all that is in the world, the lust of the flesh, and the lust of the eyes, and the pride of life, is not of the Father, but is of the world** (1 John 2:16).

The strange woman, like the **great whore, which did corrupt the earth with her fornication** (Revelation 19:2) is a temptress in the employ of Satan. Like Satan, she offers sensual pleasures that sully and defile. Those who **go astray** from God and "defile themselves" (Ezekiel 14:11 LXX) with her will suffer **the vengeance of eternal fire** (Jude 1:7).

The wise—the saved in Christ—have identified the world and the things of it as the darkness and doom wherein Satan has laid his deadly traps. In wisdom, they keep their hearts from turning aside to the ways of the strange woman (Proverbs 7:25 LXX). It is for this reason that although we are to be "in the world" as ambassadors for the kingdom of heaven, we are never to be "of the world".

We symbolically enter the home of the strange woman and defile ourselves with her when we are so tempted by what she offers that we must "buy". We buy worldliness into our hearts, minds, and homes when we fail to set our affection wholly on Christ in faithfulness and love. The errant and the lost seek and consume sensual pleasures that are created by Satan to entice and entrap us. This chapter describes what those enticements are.

Although this chapter deals specifically with the wanton woman, it can also be read as a metaphor wherein she represents Satan. Her prey, the "senseless ones" are those who are weak in faith, weak in knowledge, and weak in Spirit.

Profile #4: The Wanton Woman
Gone Astray in a Spirit of Whoredom (Hosea 4:12 LXX)
THE PROVERBS 7 WOMAN

The words of Solomon to his son:

> Say that wisdom is thy sister, and gain prudence as an acquaintance for thyself; that she may keep thee from the strange and wicked woman, if she should assail thee with flattering words. For she looks from a window out of her house into the streets, at one whom she may see of the senseless ones, a young man void of understanding, passing by the corner in the passages near her house, and speaking, in the dark of the evening, when there happens to be the stillness of night and of darkness: and the woman meets him having the appearance of a harlot, that causes the hearts of young men to flutter.
>
> And she is fickle, and debauched, and her feet abide not at home. For at one time she wanders without, and at another time she lies in wait in the streets, at every corner.
>
> Then she caught him, and kissed him, and with an impudent face said to him, I have a peace-offering; today I pay my vows: therefore I came forth to meet thee, desiring thy face; and I have found thee. I have spread my bed with sheets, and I have covered it with double tapestry from Egypt. I have sprinkled my couch with saffron, and my house with cinnamon. Come, and let us enjoy love until the morning; come, and let us embrace in love. For my husband is not at home, but is gone on a long journey, having taken in his hand a bundle of money: after many days he will return to his house.

So with much converse she prevailed on him to go astray, and with the snares of her lips forced him from the right path. And he followed her, being gently led on, and that as an ox is led to the slaughter, and as a dog to bonds, or as a hart[9] shot in the liver with an arrow: and he hastens as a bird into a snare, not knowing that he is running for his life.

Now then, my son, hearken to me, and attend to the words of my mouth. Let not thine heart turn aside to her ways: for she has wounded and cast down many, and those whom she has slain are innumerable. Her house is the way of hell, leading down to the chambers of death (Proverbs 7:4-27 LXX paragraph breaks mine).

How Does a Woman Reveal Herself as Wanton?

In general terms, wanton means unrestrained and gratuitous. Biblically, the word implies covetous, lustful, and selfish actions that accompany worldly-mindedness.[10] An empty vessel, as a woman, is "wanton" because she is interminably unsatisfied, in a constant state of "want", and unfulfilled. Therefore, she is perpetually on the hunt (Proverbs 6:26 LXX). The Bible describes her actions in the following terms: **thou didst go a-whoring, and was not satisfied** (Ezekiel 16:28 LXX). This is the definition of the wanton woman.

The reason that this is so dangerous is because by trying to fill herself up on the things of this world, the wanton woman has proven herself to be a follower of the world rather than a follower of God (1 John 2:15). Not only is this idolatry, but for the believing woman, it is adultery (James 4:4).

A wanton woman reveals herself when she desires wealth, glory, and prosperity to be consumed not by her soul in eternal life, but by her mortal body in the here and now (James 4:3-4). She proves herself to be worldly in the following ways: she is 1) manipulative, 2) fickle, 3) debauched, and 4) impudent.

---

[9]   A hart is a deer.
[10]   James 5:5, 2 Peter 2:18

Many of these devices do not come naturally to Christian women but are conveyed and suggested to us through the secular media (via the prince of the power of the air). Because we are for the most part unaware of how much we have been influenced not only by what we see around us, but by what we read, this is probably the most important chapter in this book, as well as the most difficult to hear.

1) Manipulative.

And I find her to be, and I will pronounce to be more bitter than death the woman which is a snare, and her heart nets, who has a band in her hands (Ecclesiastes 7:26a LXX). A wanton woman uses manipulation to get her way. The tactics she uses are commonly referred to as feminine wiles. A wile, when employed for the purposes of manipulation, is a deceitful charm, a duplicitous and exploitative behaviour used to entice or beguile. A woman who wields such devices is a snare; she lays traps for men who often do not escape once they have been caught therein. Solomon entreats his son to stay away from such a woman: **Let not thine heart turn aside to her ways: for she hath wounded many, and those whom she has slain are innumerable** (Proverbs 7:25-26 LXX). Utter ruination awaits the man who falls into her trap. Even strong men who allow their egos to be stroked by her honeyed tongue (Proverbs 5:3 LXX) do not resist her. Their lack of discernment will lead to their deaths. The **young man void of understanding** (Proverbs 7:6b LXX) is easy prey for such a woman.

There are wise men and women of integrity that can, by God's grace and power, resist the wiles of the manipulator. Joseph, for example, refused Potiphar's wife's invitation, saying, **how shall I do this wicked thing, and sin against God?** (Genesis 39:9b LXX). I pray that you are, or will one day be married to such a man as this.

In this section, I will deconstruct the following devices or feminine wiles: a) flattery, b) physical persuasion, c) emotional persuasion, and d) mystique.

a) Flattery

A wanton woman uses sweet, lying words and fraudulent praises to lure others. **Give no heed to a worthless woman; for honey drops from the lips of a harlot, who for a season pleases thy palate** (Proverbs 5:2-3 LXX). She is on the attack when she uses flattery. Solomon warns his son against **the strange and wicked woman, if she should *assail* thee with flattering words** (Proverbs 7:5 LXX, emphasis mine). The heart of man has little will to resist the counterfeit reverence provided by flattering lips. **A man is tried by the mouth of them that praise him** (Proverbs 27:21 LXX). Put those flattering lips on a woman, and a man's good sense may waver.

The Proverbs 7 woman said to the unwise young man, **I came forth to meet thee, desiring thy face; and I have found thee** (Proverbs 7:15b LXX). What she "found" was a senseless young man, the kind of prey for which a huntress is on the prowl. Proverbs 6 also speaks of such a woman: **For the value of a harlot is as much as one loaf; and a woman hunts for the precious souls of men** (Proverbs 6:26 LXX). The same **strange and wicked** woman from (Proverbs 7:5 LXX), **with the snares of her lips forced [the senseless one] from the right path** (Proverbs 7:21 LXX).

The scriptures teach us that flattery is both wicked and violent. It is a snare or a trap. As a form of manipulation, it is characterized by insincerity and covetousness. Paul wrote, **For neither at any time used we flattering words, as ye know, nor a cloke of covetousness; God is witness** (1 Thessalonians 2:5). The flatterer has an ulterior, corrupt motive.

Some **by good words and fair speeches deceive the hearts of the simple** (Romans 16:18b). If you have ever been the victim of a manipulative flatterer, you will have walked away from an encounter having lost your moral ground, wondering where your integrity went. You may even fall prey to another woman. Her interest is selfish gain by flattering your senses into numbness and by disarming the critical filter of your mind. Following such an encounter, you feel sullied and used. It is because you have been flattered into doing something against your better judgment. Flattery is a violent attack against the conscience; it stupefies our ability to discern right from wrong. It undermines the work of the Holy Spirit.

Deuteronomy 29 gives us an example of the effect of flattery on the mind. After the Lord warns the Israelites about the curses that will come upon them if they disobey His laws, He says

> **And it shall be if one shall hear the words of this curse, and shall flatter himself in his heart, saying, Let good happen to me, for I will walk in the error of my heart, lest the sinner destroy the guiltless with him: God shall by no means be willing to pardon him, but then the wrath of the Lord and his jealousy shall flame out against that man; and all the curses of this covenant shall attach themselves to him, which are written in this book, and the Lord shall blot out his name from under heaven** (Deuteronomy 29:19-20 LXX).

Sometimes we flatter ourselves in our own hearts. This nullifies the good work of the conscience and is inexcusable before God.

He that reproves a man's ways shall have more favour than he that flatters with the tongue (Proverbs 28:23 LXX). It is far more important to give a friend the truth, knowing that it may injure her, than to resort to a half-truth cloaked in flattery. Remember that flattery perpetrates violence against the conscience. It is far more damaging than the truth. If your best friend flatters you, beware. By failing to tell you the truth in love, she is assisting you to deceive your own heart and be willingly ignorant. **The wounds of a friend are more to be trusted than the spontaneous kisses of an enemy** (Proverbs 27:6 LXX).

One Christian author wrote that flattery between Christian women is "pure". Not so. Flattery doesn't earn but steals immediate trust and likeability from a stranger, creating a fake first impression. This device serves to make fast friends with someone without having to prove your character first. Often, friendships forged in this manner are precarious and shallow. If you want to forge a godly friendship, choose to use words that edify the listener in Christ (Ephesians 4:29). Love with sincerity (Romans 12:9) and speak with grace (Colossians 4:6). **Let love be without dissimulation.**[11] **Abhor that which is evil; cleave to that which is good** (Romans 12:9).

---

[11] Dissimulation is insincerity.

A flatterer's **throat is an open sepulchre; with their tongues they have used deceit; the poison of asps is under their lips** (Romans 3:13). With it, she will lead her prey down to the **chambers of death** (Proverbs 7:27b LXX). Flattery has no place in either the inner workings of a Christian's heart or in the outer workings of Christian fellowship. It is the device of a manipulator.

b) Physical persuasion

A wanton woman uses her outward appearance, or physical attributes, to seduce a man. **Let not the desire of beauty overcome thee, neither be thou caught by thine eyes, neither be captivated with her eyelids** (Proverbs 6:25 LXX). The physical cues of sensuality do not go unnoticed by the average man, nor by the high-minded intellectual. No man knew this better than Solomon. A flutter of the eyelids, a dilated pupil, a protruding hip, or a lingering touch of the finger to the mouth or hair—all are registered by a man's visual cortex as a sexual cue. All have the power to create physical persuasion. Like the "great whore" of Revelation 19:2, **which did corrupt the earth with her fornication**, today's secular media uses this device as its primary method of advertising. **For they that are after the flesh do mind the things of the flesh; but they that are after the Spirit, the things of the Spirit. For to be carnally minded is death: but to be spiritually minded is life and peace** (Romans 8:6-7a). A wanton woman is hyper-aware of her physicality and uses it as a means of manipulation. **And the woman meets him having the appearance of a harlot, that causes the hearts of young men to flutter** (Proverbs 7:10 LXX). Her boldness in this area elicits shock value, and provokes an instinctive reaction in the man. **Then she caught him, and kissed him, and with an impudent face said . . .** (Proverbs 7:13a LXX). When a man's resistance is down, and a physical reaction is forced on him through touch, **he hastens as a bird into a snare, not knowing that he is running for his life** (Proverbs 7:23 LXX).

Some Christian women mimic these physical gestures without knowing it. If you expose yourself to secular music videos, fashion shows, or television/movies, you may have taken on gestures that have been mapped on to you unawares. Ask a trusted friend to be your accountability partner, pointing out to you ways that you may be communicating sexual cues without realizing it.

A godly woman moves with grace and poise. She is demure and confident. These are not skills to be learned from the world; they are the outward expressions of a godly, pure mind. To get them, **Set your affection on things above, not on things on the earth** (Colossians 3:2).

c) Emotional persuasion

Delilah said to Sampson, **Behold, thou hast deceived me, and told me lies; tell me, I intreat thee, wherewith thou mayest be bound** (Judges 16:13 LXX). When her gentle entreaties failed for the third time in a row, she changed tactics. She said,

> **How sayest thou, I love thee, when thy heart is not with me? this third time thou hast deceived me, and hast not told me wherein is thy great strength. And it came to pass as she pressed him sore with her words continually, and straitened him, that his spirit failed almost to death. Then he told her all his heart** (Judges 16:15-17a LXX).

Delilah hired herself out as a harlot for the purpose of beguiling Samson. She was paid 1100 pieces of silver by each of the Philistine princes (Judges 16:5 LXX).

Like Delilah, a wanton woman persuades with emotional manipulation. She bullies and oppresses her victim with the passion and tirelessness of strong feelings. **It is better to dwell in the wilderness than with a quarrelsome and talkative and passionate[12] woman** (Proverbs 21:19 LXX).

A passionate woman such as this is driven by her emotions to get her own way. She presses her point home to a man tirelessly and incessantly until he cannot rest without giving in. Like Delilah, she will allege that his

---

[12]   The word "passionate" here denotes strong feelings that can change unpredictably such as love/hate or anger/joy. Such emotional extremes can only be tempered by obedience to Christ and the subsequent use of His power to help quell them.

unwillingness to do her will is "proof" that he does not love her. Her most effective tactic is to shed the false tears of an "unloved" woman, effectively playing the victim while painting him as the villain. Eventually she will break his will. He will be forced to do what she wants, even if what she wants defies reason, even if what she wants is selfish, vain, or immoral, and even if what she wants is contrary to the will of God. These are the tactics of a manipulative woman. **So with much converse she prevailed on him to go astray** (Proverbs 7:21a LXX).

For she goes not upon the paths of life; but her ways are slippery, and not easily known (Proverbs 5:6 LXX). A manipulative woman can be a slippery snake. In a show of emotional weakness or neediness, she will convince her victim that she is being used, despised, abused, ignored, or misunderstood. Her emotional distress mitigates moral reality. She will use it to deceive her victim into believing that she is unable to fulfill her social, marital, Christian, civic, or parental obligations. She is not incapable; she is unwilling. Her false display of vulnerability is a deceitful pretence—a form of manipulation.

Charms are false, and woman's beauty is vain (Proverbs 31:30 LXX). Vulnerability can be beautiful to a man. It triggers his protective instincts. The wanton woman uses this to her advantage, but if she fails to get her way, she will become a venomous snake. She will slander, backstab, and accuse falsely with a poisonous bite. **And I find her to be and I pronounce to be more bitter than death the woman which is a snare, and her heart nets** (Ecclesiastes 7:26 LXX).

Several years ago, my mother confided to me that she had stopped reading romance novels. She said that they made her emotional, effecting her mood and disposition. I was never much for reading romance novels, I must confess, but shortly thereafter, I joined a book club and had to read one. Like clockwork, the morning after I read the first few chapters, I was moody and irritable, unpleasant and unsatisfied. I was upset with my husband over something trivial and vain. After much consternation, wondering what had happened to "pleasant Paige", I finally realized that the words that came out of my mouth in complaint to my husband were almost word-for-word the very ones I had just read in the book.

This is how the secular media works. Be aware of the fact that your reactions are never entirely your own. Just as clever advertising programs anticipate purchasing patterns based on mood and emotion, so do clever theatrical re-enactments dictate to you your thoughts and behaviours. Be wise enough to avoid these ungodly influences: **Shall anyone bind fire in his bosom, and not burn his garments? or will any one walk on coals of fire, and not burn his feet?** (Proverbs 6:27-28 LXX). Protect yourself from the influence of the world—the strange, seductive, wanton woman—by filling your eyes, your heart, and your mind with the words and actions of your heavenly Father.

d) Mystique

Then Jesus said unto them, Yet a little while is the light with you. Walk while ye have the light, lest darkness come upon you: for he that walketh in darkness knoweth not whither he goeth (John 12:35). Mystique is created by an atmosphere of darkness, secrecy, or mystery. A person who uses mystique inspires awe and is often venerated as a result.

A wanton woman who targets her prey seeks the most favourable setting for her trap. Because she is relying on trickery, she will operate in the dim light. Her features will appear softer, and the shadows will create mystery and awe. Inhibitions are lowered in the evening, when men are tired. **For she looks from a window out of her house into the streets, at one whom she may see of the senseless ones, a young man void of understanding, passing by the corner in the passages near her house, and speaking, in the dark of the evening, when there happens to be the stillness of night and of darkness** (Proverbs 7:6-9 LXX). That which is hidden, or performed under cover of darkness, is often deceitful. Those whose intentions are impure rely on the darkness to conceal their sin. **Men loved darkness rather than light, because their deeds were evil** (John 3:19b).

When the wanton woman catches the senseless man's attention, she builds further mystique by painting an anticipatory picture in his mind. She appeals to his sensual imagination by describing the Egyptian tapestry draping her bed and the scents of saffron and cinnamon on her couch and in her house, then saying, **Come, and let us enjoy love until the morning; come, and let us embrace in love** (Proverbs 7:18 LXX). She has purposefully associated the powerful senses of scent, sight, and touch with the act of love-making. The trap is set.

Once his senses have been titillated, she overcomes his objections. She explains that her husband has **gone on a long journey** (Proverbs 7:19b LXX).[13] The senseless young man now thinks that he will be safe from discovery. He will have many days to enjoy her home. **And he followed her being gently led on . . . and he hastens as a bird into a snare, not knowing that he is running for his life** (Proverbs 7:22a, 23b LXX).

2) Fickle.

A wanton woman is disloyal. Disloyalty is a qualifying definition for the word "fickle". Because a wanton woman feels no particular allegiance to any one thing, she flits about whimsically, with no set course, giving her loyalty away cheaply, to anything or anyone at all. **And she is fickle, and debauched, and her feet abide not at home. For at one time she wanders without, and at another time she lies in wait in the streets, at every corner** (Proverbs 7:11-12 LXX). Because she heeds no particular doctrine and changes her mind with the breeze, she lacks direction and is restless. She stands for nothing, so she accepts anything. **A double minded man is unstable in all his ways** (James 1:8).

A stable, godly woman sets her path firmly in Christ. She has confidence, conviction, and security. Worldly whims have no appeal to her.

I remember being on a long airplane flight and watching a movie about a young girl who wanted to save all her money to go to Paris. When her parents lamented the cost, her emotional reply was, "But I need to *find* myself"! The parents relented, the girl went off to Paris, found "true love", and returned home beaming with happiness. The story always ends there. We are not told about the next whim she will have when the honeymoon

---

13   It is no coincidence that in Matthew 25:14-15, the lord in the parable "called his own servants, and delivered unto them his goods…. and straightway took his journey". Verse 19 says, "After a long time the lord of those servants cometh, and reckoneth with them". It matters very much what you do while the Lord Jesus Christ is away. Will you be faithful?

is over and she wants something or someone new. We are not shown the disastrous results of living a fickle, unstable life.

There is only one reason a person feels the need to "find herself". It is because she has not found Christ. With Christ, we are identified, defined, and secured in and through Him. He is the treasure for which we forsake all—including the imaginations of our hearts—to keep. Once this treasure is secured, none other is required.

Movies like this (and there are many) ensnare fickle women whose identity is not secure in Christ. These movies are seductive traps set by **the rulers of the darkness of this world** (Ephesians 6:12) through the secular media. Caught therein are many young Christian girls who, at the age of about 15, have a sudden and acute desire to go on a "mission trip".

Remember that the Proverbs 7 woman's **feet abide not at home . . . she wanders without . . .** (Proverbs 7:11-12 LXX). The Proverbs 7 woman is fickle. She is wandering about because she is unsatisfied and discontent. She is not a "keeper at home" (Titus 2:5). A 15 year-old girl pining to go on a mission trip differs little from the Proverbs 7 woman whose carnal lusts propel her out to "see and be seen". Young girls (and older ones) are running on hormones that are exacerbated by the secular media's glorification of worldly-mindedness (in this case exotic travel). These young girls leave busy households and exhausted mothers behind so that they can do something for *themselves*. Although they assert that they are wholly motivated by their heart-felt desire to "do something for God", God has little to do with it, becoming nothing more than a proffered "moral justification" that few parents are equipped enough to disprove.

Please don't get me wrong. I am not speaking against mission work as prescribed in Proverbs 31 and exemplified by godly, Titus 2 women such as Priscilla (Acts 18) or Deborah (Judges 4), whom we will learn about later. I am speaking against the fickle desires demonstrated by the spiritually immature who do not realize that they are being influenced by "higher powers" (Ephesians 6:12). Often well-meaning women, old and young, are led by the "imaginations of their hearts"[14] and do not realize that these "imaginations" are vain, impure and misguided. For this reason, Solomon

---

[14]   Genesis 6:5, 8:24, Deuteronomy 29:19, 1 Chronicles 28:9, Jeremiah 3:17, 7:24, 9:14, 11:8, 16:12, 18:12, 23:17, Luke 1:51, Romans 1:21

tells his son to **be wise, and rightly direct the thoughts of thine heart** (Proverbs 23:19 LXX).

Lofty dreams and imaginations that are contrary to the Word of God tend to be informed or exacerbated by the secular media. They lead astray the unstable. Instead of allowing the allures of the world and the vanity of our hearts to thwart our **good conversation in Christ** (1 Peter 3:16), choose to **gird up the loins of your mind, [and] be sober** (1 Peter 1:13a). Rest assured that being a "keeper at home" (Titus 2:5), "obedient to your own husband" (Titus 2:5), or your own parent (Colossians 3:20), may not be glorious in the eyes of the world, but it is God's will for you, considered of the utmost value to Him. It is the straight path, which is embarked upon out of faithfulness and loyalty to the Most High God.

3) Debauched.

But she that liveth in pleasure is dead while she liveth (1 Timothy 5:6). A debauched woman is carnal; she is addicted to sensual pleasure. Sensual pleasures are the lusts of the flesh.

> **Now the works of the flesh are manifest, which are these; Adultery, fornication, uncleanness, lasciviousness, Idolatry, witchcraft, hatred, variance, emulations, wrath, strife, seditions, heresies, Envyings, murders, drunkenness, revellings, and such like: of the which I tell you before, as I have also told you in time past, that they which do such things shall not inherit the kingdom of God** (Galatians 5:19-21).

As you can see, lust and sensual pleasures refer to far more than fornication and adultery; they include covetousness, wantonness and all the desires of the flesh, which are the desires of this world.

> **Love not the world, neither the things that are in the world. If any man love the world, the love of the Father is not in him. For all that is in the world, the lust of the flesh, and the lust of the eyes, and the pride of life, is not of the Father, but is of the world** (1 John 2:15-16).

A wanton woman seeks and finds fleshly pleasure in the things of the world. As such, she is cheating on God. **Ye adulterers and adulteresses, know ye not that the friendship of the world is enmity with God? whosoever therefore will be a friend to the world is the enemy of God** (James 4:4).

Jesus said, **My kingdom is not of this world** (John 18:36a). The **prince of this world** (John 12:31), or the **god of this world** (2 Corinthians 4:4), is the devil, and the things of this world are his snares, set to enslave us. A wanton woman believes that her choice to be worldly reflects her freedom. On the contrary, it reflects the fact that she is in the snare of the devil, and has been **taken captive by him at his will** (2 Timothy 2:26). She is a slave to sin and is under bondage, but she believes herself free. **While they promise them liberty, they themselves are the servants of corruption: for of whom a man is overcome, of the same is he brought in bondage** (2 Peter 2:19). The enticements of the world **allure through the lusts of the flesh, and through much wantonness** (2 Peter 2:18) and have thereby seduced and entrapped her in bondage. **So then they that are in the flesh cannot please God** (Romans 8:8). For this reason, she is described as being dead while she lives (1 Timothy 5:6).

But ye are not in the flesh, but in the Spirit, if so be that the Spirit of God dwell in you. Now if any man have not the Spirit of Christ, he is none of his (Romans 8:9). A wanton woman lives and walks in the flesh, and her flesh is her god. But **He that soweth to the Spirit shall of the Spirit reap life everlasting** (Galatians 6:8).

4) Impudent.

Then she caught him, and kissed him, and with an impudent face said unto him, I have a peace offering; today I pay my vows (Proverbs 7:13 LXX). A wanton woman is impudent, which means shameless. Shame is the capacity for feeling the distress or humiliation that accompanies a violated conscience. **Thou hadst a whore's face, thou didst become shameless toward all** (Jeremiah 3:3b LXX). Shamelessness is exhibited through immodesty.

Immodesty is revealed in many observable ways. The outward expression of it broadcasts the state of the heart with alarming clarity.

In general, a wanton woman lacks restraint. She has a rusty conscience; one that has not been oiled or worked often enough to run smoothly. The longer she ignores it, the more the rust will eat away at the good parts. Eventually, it will not run at all.

Quench not the Spirit (1 Thessalonians 5:19). Shamelessness results from a quenched spirit: or a "defiled conscience".[15] A wanton woman walks around advertising to all who can see that her conscience is in desperate need of a tune-up. Her immodesty is revealed most clearly by: a) the way she dresses, and b) the way she talks.

a) The way she dresses

[And] the woman meets him having the appearance of a harlot (Proverbs 7:10a LXX). One day, a pastor's wife was arrested for prostitution. A police officer saw her walking down the street in a seedy part of town at night. She looked like a "harlot", so he assumed her to be one and arrested her.[16]

A wise man once told my husband and me the old adage, "If you're not in the business, don't advertise". What does your outward appearance advertise? Do you have "the appearance of a harlot", or do you adorn yourself **in modest apparel, with shamefacedness and sobriety** (1Timothy 2:9b)?

It is a shame to be uncovered, and a wanton woman is uncovered. The words "naked" and "shamed" are used interchangeably in the Old Testament Septuagint (LXX) and King James versions of the Bible, but only in reference to the adulteress. For example, **she exposed her fornication and exposed her shame** (Ezekiel 23:18 LXX); **she discovered her whoredoms and discovered her nakedness** (Ezekiel 23:18 KJV). When the Septuagint says, **they uncovered her shame**, the King James says, **they discovered her nakedness.**[17] Shame and nakedness are one and the same.

---

[15]   Titus 1:15, 1 Corinthians 8:7

[16]   From Dr. S. M. Davis; a CD entitled "The Language of the Christian's Clothing".

[17]   These references include all the nations that are likened to the "whore" as well as particular people such as the Proverbs 7 woman: Ezekiel 16:36, 37, 22:10, 23:10, 18, 29, Nahum 3:5 LXX/KJV

In the Garden of Eden, when Adam and Eve became cognizant of their sin, the first action they took was to cover themselves. This was a direct reaction to their awareness of sin. Sin evokes shame and the accompanying desire to hide. **For in this we groan, earnestly desiring to be clothed upon with our house which is from heaven: If so be that being clothed we shall not be found naked** (2 Corinthians 5:2-3). A wanton woman is found naked. Biblically speaking, there is no greater shame. It is the same as having your sin exposed, revealing to all that the blood of Jesus Christ is not yours as a covering.

Behold, I am against thee, saith the Lord God Almighty, and I will uncover thy skirts in thy presence, and I will shew the nations thy shame, and the kingdoms thy disgrace (Nahum 3:5 LXX). The Lord, in speaking of Jerusalem, promises to expose her sin and her shame. Her problem was that she was walking around as though she had none. This is the state of our current society. If you leave your home only to find the streets filled with an assortment of scantily clad individuals, it is because there is sin without shame, **having their conscience seared with a hot iron** (1 Timothy 4:2). **Such is the way of an adulterous woman, who having washed herself from what she has done, says she has done nothing amiss** (Proverbs 30:20 LXX).

A woman of conscience acknowledges sin in her life and exhibits the desire to cover herself. She dresses modestly, and she exhibits a humble and demure attitude, aware of her sin and of her need for a Saviour. Such **women adorn themselves . . . not with broided hair, or gold, or pearls, or costly array; But (which becometh women professing godliness) with good works** (1 Timothy 2:9-10). Her good deeds are a reflection of the gratitude she has in her heart for being washed by the blood of Jesus. She walks around covered, not only in the literal sense, but in the sense that the blood of Christ has covered her sin. She has no need of gold or pearls, of fancy hairstyles or the latest fashion trends. What she has as her covering is invaluable. **But let it be the hidden man of the heart, in that which is not corruptible, even the ornament of a meek and quiet spirit, which is in the sight of God of great price** (1 Peter 3:4).

From head to toe, what you put on matters. **But put ye on the Lord Jesus Christ, and make not provision for the flesh, to fulfill the lusts thereof** (Romans 13:14). When we have put on Christ, we are purposing to conduct ourselves in a manner befitting of His Name, as His dear children. With diligence, we strive to do as Paul says in Romans 12: **And be not conformed to this world: but be ye transformed by the renewing of your mind, that ye may prove what is that good, and acceptable, and perfect, will of God** (Romans 12:2). Making a provision for the flesh means that we have set our minds on the things of this world, lusting after impotent gods. Such idol worship is an act of war against the soul: **abstain from fleshly lusts, which war against the soul** (1 Peter 2:11).

And I will recompense on her the days of Baalim, wherein she sacrificed to them, and put on her ear-rings, and her necklaces, and went after her lovers, and forgot me, saith the Lord (Hosea 2:13 LXX). Today, the lovers she sacrifices her good sense and pocket book for include brand named clothing, post-modernist humanism,[18] a "Sex in the City" lifestyle,[19] or false virtue that is predicated upon compromised Christianity. What these all have in common is that they promote violence against the soul through self-worship. **Therefore, brethren, we are debtors, not to the flesh, to live after the flesh. For if ye live after the flesh, ye shall die: but if ye through the Spirit do mortify the deeds of the body, ye shall live** (Romans 8:13-14). These are false gods and false doctrines that are "put on" by a wanton, immodest woman.

I have been to many churches where women dress provocatively, without shame. It is lamentable that the average woman on the street dresses no differently from a prostitute, but the fact that a woman professing the name of Jesus Christ as her Lord and Saviour can be mistaken for one is a profound tragedy. If you profess the name of Jesus Christ as your Lord and Saviour, cover up from your neck to your knees.[20]

---

[18] These philosophies promote the relativity of truth, the elevation of man over God, absolute tolerance (which is an intolerance of intolerance - oxymoronic), and self-determination (unlimited by the "confines" of "oppressive" Biblical authority).

[19] This syndicated television show features single, adult women engaging in promiscuous sex, promoting it as a form of female empowerment, while glorifying and reveling in immodesty.

[20] I recommend Dr. S. M. Davis's instructive 2-CD set entitled "The Language of the Christian's Clothing".

b) The way she talks

One summer, my husband and I visited England with our two boys. We did what tourists do; we rode a red, double-decker tour bus through London proper. After several stops, a new tour guide arrived. She was a middle-aged, attractive woman who started off quite well, telling us what all good tourists like to hear. All of a sudden, things got ugly. She began to tell a bus load of complete strangers gory details about her personal life. Soon we knew her sexual history, her financial woes, and her family quarrels. *It was the same as if she had been removing all her clothes.* We were off that bus at the first opportunity. She vocalized that which was meant to be kept private. She had no shame and no restraint. **Life and death are in the power of the tongue; and they that rule it shall eat the fruits thereof** (Proverbs 18:21 LXX).

A good man out of the good treasure of his heart bringeth forth that which is good; and an evil man out of the evil treasure of his heart bringeth forth that which is evil: for of the abundance of the heart his mouth speaketh (Luke 6:45). Paul, in his letter to the Ephesians wrote, **And have no fellowship with the unfruitful works of darkness, but rather reprove them. For it is a shame even to speak of those things which are done of them in secret** (Ephesians 5:11-12).

A wanton woman speaks flippantly about sin. She will recount to her friends the details of her sexual encounters, vicariously subjecting them to the same filth in which she revels. Every time she talks about it, she relives the sin and in a way commits it afresh. She tells the story with pride, attempting to make her debauchery seem normal, acceptable, even enviable. **My son, envy not bad men, nor desire to be with them. For their heart meditates falsehoods, and their lips speak mischiefs** (Proverbs 24:1-2 LXX).

STUDY BREAK
A Vessel Full of Holes

Biblically, a vessel is a carrying pot, or pitcher. It can also refer to a person. Some vessels are more honourable than others.[21] They are made of

---

21   Romans 9:21, 2 Timothy 2:20-21

differing material: some clay, some earthen, some of brass, silver, or gold (2 Timothy 2:20). Some vessels are consecrated to the Lord (Joshua 6:18-19 LXX). Others are dedicated to Baal (2 Kings 23:4 LXX).

There are "overseers of the vessels", "vessels for ministration of the service" and "vessels for the house of the Lord".[22] Vessels can be defiled, in which case, they must be sanctified and returned to their rightful place.[23] Once a vessel is dedicated to God, it is holy (Ezra 8:28 LXX).

People, like vessels, can be broken. King David lamented in Psalm 31:12 LXX that he had become "as a broken vessel". In Jeremiah 19, God says he **will break in pieces this people, and this city, even as an earthen vessel is broken in pieces which cannot be mended again** (Jeremiah 19:11). The city He referred to was the adulterous harlot, Jerusalem.

In Matthew 25, the wise virgins took oil in their vessels, indicating that they were always inwardly prepared for the return of Christ. In Romans 9, Paul identifies that God **endured with much longsuffering the vessels of wrath fitted to destruction: And that he might make known the riches of his glory on the vessels of mercy, which he had afore prepared unto glory** (Romans 9:22b-23). Are you seeing the beauty of this pitcher?

In 1 Thessalonians 4:4, every man is told to **possess his vessel in sanctification and honour**. In 1 Peter 3:7, husbands are told to give **honour unto the wife, as unto the weaker vessel**. This "pitcher" is still beautiful.

Weaker vessels are earthen, vulnerable, and breakable. When they are honoured, sanctified and cleansed, they can be invaluable. **But we have this treasure in earthen vessels, that the excellency of the power may be of God, and not of us** (2 Corinthians 4:7). When a weak vessel carries within her the sanctifying blood of Jesus Christ, she is a vessel unto honour, a vessel which the Lord's strength makes useful. Dishonoured, defiled, or unclean vessels break apart into pieces and feel unwanted, unloved, and useless: **as the vessels of the potter shall they be broken to shivers** (Revelation 2:27).

But God accepts the broken spirit and the contrite heart. King David prayed **Wash me thoroughly from mine iniquity, and cleanse me from my sin. For I am conscious of my iniquity and my sin is continually**

---

[22]   1 Chronicles 28:13 LXX, 2 Chronicles 24:14 LXX
[23]   Joshua 6:19 LXX, Ezra 6:5 LXX

before me (Psalm 51:2-3 LXX). God cleanses us. Cleansed vessels are purged, **sanctified, and meet for the master's use** (2 Timothy 2:21). These are those who have shed the lusts of the flesh which defile them in order to set themselves apart from this world as holy and undefiled. They walk in the Spirit. They have the mind of Christ. They are made whole and invulnerable. **But if the Spirit of him that raised up Jesus from the dead dwell in you, he that raised up Christ from the dead shall also quicken your mortal bodies by his Spirit that dwelleth in you . . . For as many are led by the Spirit of God, they are the sons of God** (Romans 8:11, 14). They are unblemished, without spot or wrinkle. Be like them!

Why a Vessel Full of Holes?

For a strange house is a vessel full of holes; and a strange well is narrow (Proverbs 23:27 LXX). A strange house and a strange well refer to a strange woman and what she offers. In this chapter, we learned that although at first she seems sweet and compelling, afterward she is **more bitter than death** (Ecclesiastes 7:26 LXX) because hers is **the way of hell** (Proverbs 7:27 LXX).

A vessel full of holes is perpetually emptying; it cannot hold water. No matter how much is put into it, it is never full. **Ye have sown much, but brought in little; ye have eaten, and are not satisfied; ye have drunk, and are not satisfied with drink, ye have clothed yourselves, and have not become warm thereby: and he that earns wages has gathered them into a bag full of holes** (Haggai 1:6 LXX). This is why covetousness and wantonness mark the worldly-minded woman. She consumes the things of the world—trying on different religions just as she tries on different clothes—looking to them for meaning and fulfillment, but they are not there to be found. **A full soul scorns honeycombs; but to a hungry soul even bitter things appear sweet** (Proverbs 27:7 LXX). A "full soul" is filled up on the things of Christ, leaving her in want of nothing. A "hungry soul" does not know Christ and therefore feels perpetually empty.

There is no fulfillment in the life of a woman who lives outside the will of God. No matter how much she searches, seeks, consumes, and gathers, sooner or later, she comes up empty. She is dead while she lives. If you feel the despair of an unfulfilled life, finding that you are spinning your wheels in a futile effort to find lasting joy, put away the things of this world, and put on Christ; **If so be that being clothed we shall not be found naked** (2 Corinthians 5:3). **And now, brethren, I commend you to God, and to the word of his grace, which is able to build you up, and to give you an inheritance among all them which are sanctified** (Acts 20:32).

2 Kings 4 tells of a widow woman, a daughter of the prophets, whose faithful husband had died and whose debts were high. All that remained was the oil she used to anoint herself with as an act of devotion to the Lord. Elisha told her to borrow from her neighbours as many empty vessels as she could find and to pour what oil she had left into them. When she began to pour oil, she found that the flagon never ran dry. She poured and poured, and each vessel was filled to the brim. She sold what oil she could, paid her debts, and lived on what remained.

The widow woman, like her vessels, was filled up. She is the opposite of the wanton woman. Because she lived according to the will of God, she was blessed, and her blessings never ran out. Her vessel was one of sanctification and honour, well-pleasing in the sight of the Lord and devoted to His use. Be chaste, be loyal, and please be unwavering in your devotion to the Most High God. **For the commandment of the law is a lamp and a light; a way of life** (Proverbs 6:23a LXX).

Modern Snapshot
TRACY

One day, many years ago now, my husband-to-be and I were attending a dinner party at a friend's house. Half-way through the dinner, an unexpected guest arrived. It was a woman. She was pretty, with bleached-blonde, straightened hair and perfect make-up. She wore a dusty rose, suede skirt-suit with three-inch heels and a scarf. She wore expensive gold jewellery on her ears, neck, wrist, and fingers. She had long, painted and manicured fingernails holding a designer handbag. From the moment she entered the room, everyone's attention was on her. She poured out her life story to everyone in the room. She had recently divorced, left her kids with a sitter because she could not handle them, and "just had to get out of the house". She couldn't stay long, though, because she had other people to see and other things to do.

Unrestrained and shameless, she boasted of her failings and broadcast her indiscretions. She made snide comments using brazen, polluted speech.

Emotionally, she is unpredictable and volatile. If she fails to get her way, she will resort to sulking, moping, or raging until someone notices and accommodates her. There is no peace when she is around. If she is your friend and she calls you on the phone to tell you all about her latest exploits, you will feel tired and drained afterward. By listening to her tell you of her sin, you have vicariously experienced it. She uses you to enable her bad habits. As long as you listen to her and let her talk without rebuking her, you have contributed greater rusting of her conscience. If you love her, you will choose to admonish her, with humility and gentleness.

She is a hormonal train-wreck and will indiscriminately take up with men about whom she knows little. She measures her worth according to her ability to manipulate and beguile others. She gets bored easily, and moves from one man to the next, one marriage to the next, one fashion trend to the next, one diet to the next, and leaves her kids with one sitter or another, all in an endless pursuit of self-gratification and lust. Never satisfied and never fulfilled, she is **a vessel full of holes** (Proverbs 23:27 LXX).

On the way home from that dinner party, I asked my husband what he thought of her. To his credit, he stated accurately and succinctly, "She has a mouth like an open grave" (Psalm 5:9). From that day forward, I knew exactly what a wanton woman was, and now, so do you.

And thou shalt be naked and bare: and the shame of thy fornication shall be exposed (Ezekiel 23:29 LXX).

Summary

A wanton woman is not defined by her job description so much as she is defined by her lifestyle and appearance. With her words she persuades and beguiles, flatters and manipulates. She speaks without restraint or discretion. She is faithless and disloyal to God and to man. Her affection vacillates, and she is unstable in all her ways. She walks in the flesh and is a friend to the world. She is an adulteress who has no shame.

The faithful married woman is subject to one man and one God. The unmarried woman is undistracted by service to her husband and lives in singleness of mind to serve the Lord. Both women seek and find fulfillment in the family of Christ and are not swayed by the temptations of the world. They are blessed. **Wherefore, beloved, seeing that ye look for [new heavens and a new earth, wherein dwelleth righteousness], be diligent that ye may be found of him in peace, without spot, and blameless** (2 Peter 3:14).

Who Shall Deliver Me?

- **And what wilt thou do? Though thou clothe thyself with scarlet, and adorn thyself with golden ornaments; though thou adorn thine eyes with stibium, thy beauty will be in vain: thy lovers have rejected thee, they seek thy life** (Jeremiah 4:30 LXX).
- **If we say that we have no sin, we deceive ourselves, and the truth is not in us. If we confess our sins, he is faithful and just to forgive us our sins, and to cleanse us from all unrighteousness** (1 John 1:8-9).
- **For we ourselves also were sometimes . . . serving divers lusts and pleasures . . . But after that the kindness and love of God our Saviour toward man appeared, Not by works of righteousness that we have done, but according to his mercy he saved us, by the washing of regeneration, and renewing of the Holy Ghost** (Titus 3:3-5).

How Can I Be Filled?

1. Put on Christ (Romans 13:14).
2. Dress modestly and behave soberly (1 Timothy 2:9-10).
3. Strengthen your vessel (2 Thessalonians 2:17).
4. Dedicate your vessel to God (1 Thessalonians 4:4).
5. Be a keeper at home (Titus 1:2).

6.   Love your *own* husband (Ephesians 5:33).
7.   Obey your *own* husband (Titus 1:5).

Think on These Things

1.   How has God shown his faithfulness to you?
     Heb. 10:23, Rev. 1:5
2.   Do I see truth and avoid flattery?
     Rom. 16:18
3.   Am I trustworthy in all I do?
     1 Cor. 4:2, Luke 16:10
4.   How can I know the truth?
     John 16:13
5.   How can I change?
     Romans 12:2
6.   How are we to be clothed?
     Col. 3:12, 2 Cor. 5:2
7.   Do I listen to juicy stories?
     Eph. 5:11-1
8.   Why is it not degrading to be referred to as "the weaker vessel"?
     2 Cor. 4:6-7
9.   How can we be sanctified?
     1 Thess. 5:23
10. How does God adorn us?
     1 Pet. 3:3-5
11. Why should we glorify God in our bodies?
     1 Cor. 6:18-20
12. When we receive the Holy Spirit, what happens inside us?
     1 Cor. 6:19

CHAPTER FIVE

NOT ONLY IDLE

1 TIMOTHY 5:13

Introduction
Arise and Do (1 Chronicles 22:16 LXX)

I have developed a method in writing these chapters. At the beginning of each chapter, I research. I immerse myself in the Bible, searching out as many examples of the profile and its related words as possible. I check the dictionaries, old and new, to see how the use of the word has changed over time. I pray. I ask the Lord to direct my heart and show me what He would have me learn and share. Then, I sit back and wait on the Lord's leading. Sooner or later, the Holy Spirit will inspire me, and I will "arise and do."

He has been faithful. For this chapter, as I was in "wait" mode, I picked up one of my Laura Ingalls Wilder books. I have them in *queue*, as books that I wanted to read for myself before my husband and I deemed them appropriate for our children. I picked up *The Long Winter* and could hardly put it down. Then, I picked up *Little Town on the Prairie* and I couldn't put that one down either. I am currently half way through *These Happy Golden* Years.

I began to wonder if I was being idle by reading. It was far too amusing[1], and I was rushing to keep up with my daily chores. Was this the lesson that I was to learn and teach? No. This morning I woke up

---

[1]   "Amuse" literally means to not think.

inspired. As I pondered the lives of Charles and Caroline Ingalls, I realized that I *wished that I were them*, and I realized why.

There is only one way to test your mettle, and the early homesteaders knew the way. Put yourself out there. Place yourself in a situation where you must do or die. Leave no safety net. Learn how to preserve food and live off it over the winter, or starve. Cut and gather enough wood to warm you over the winter, or freeze. Rely on your ability to track, trap, or shoot meat for your family to live on. If all you have are potatoes to eat for three months, then learn how to make them interesting.

A wife in such a desperate situation can be enterprising, inventive, and useful; or she can be bitter, mopey, and useless. She can think of her hands as being too delicate to get dirty and work-worn, or she can see them as being meant to work and able to bless. Her cheerful countenance displayed in the worst of times is a statement of character. Her willingness to get out of her comfort zone to help with man's work is a sign of courage.

These are the trials that tested, shaped, and developed the character of the pioneers. These men and women of substance settled nations and formed the national character. In those days, if people didn't work hard, they paid with their lives. If they did work hard and had the tough luck to get caught in a blizzard, or fall from a rooftop, or become a victim of a railroad construction accident, they died, leaving wives and children to fend for themselves and either survive, or not.

Today, there is no do or die in our pampered, privileged society. Today, there are no sure ways to test one's mettle. In our current society, the ignoble cowards thrive alongside the brave, and few discerning eyes are able to identify them before it's too late. Even worse, those who see through their pretences are accused of intolerance and hatred for recognizing them for what they are.

In *These Happy Golden Years*, Almanzo Wilder fetches Laura from her teaching post twelve miles away in the dead of winter to bring her home to her family for the weekend. On one occasion, he considered staying home. The temperature was 40 below zero and falling. To make matters worse, the previous weekend Laura had confided to him that she was only using him for his ride. As Almanzo walked along Main Street deliberating on his decision, he saw his friend Cap Garland, with whom he had made a treacherous and selfless journey the previous winter. Together they had proven their mettle and saved the townspeople from imminent starvation.

Cap, seeing that Almanzo had not yet departed on his usual trip to fetch Laura, said to him, "God hates a coward".[2] That statement prompted Almanzo's departure; he was no coward. At first, I wondered at such a statement. Does God really hate a coward? I believe He does.

The more I thought about the Ingalls and the Wilders of the past, the more I thought about the labourers of Christ in the present. As Christians, we have opportunities every day to prove our mettle. Every day, we are called to live an uncompromising life. Every day, we are called to stand apart from the world, to diligently learn the Word, to labour for what is eternal, and to suffer persecution and hatred for the name of Christ. These things take courage.

A Christian is either prepared to stand up and defend her faith, giving an answer, or she gets caught in the blizzard of compromise, and like a coward, she tucks her tail between her legs as she fails to assert the truth of God's Word. If your life is easy and your trials few, I ask you, what have you been doing for the kingdom of God lately? My challenge to you in this chapter is this. Be a **labourer worthy of [your] hire** (Luke 10:7). **Arise and do, and the Lord be with thee** (1 Chronicles 22:16b LXX).

Profile #5: The Idle Woman
Attend Upon the Lord Without Distraction (1 Corinthians 7:35b)
THE YOUNG WIDOW

Paul's letters to Timothy included instructions for the church. 1st Timothy 5 specifies how the church is to help widows. The Bible differentiates between two types of widow. **Widows indeed** (1Timothy 5:3b) are those women over 60 years old who have no husbands and no means of providing for themselves. A woman qualifies as being a widow indeed if she is **desolate, trusteth in God, and continueth in supplications and prayers night and day** (1 Timothy 5:5).

---

[2] Laura Ingalls Wilder, *These Happy Golden Years* (New York, NY: Harper Collins Publishers, 1943), p77.

For young widows, Paul's instructions differ. These differences are the focus of this chapter. They are as follows:

> **Let not a widow be taken into the number under threescore years old, having been the wife of one man, Well reported of for good works; if she have brought up children, if she have lodged strangers, if she have washed the saints' feet, if she have relieved the afflicted, if she have diligently followed every good work.**
>
> **But the younger widows refuse: for when they have begun to wax wanton against Christ, they will marry; Having damnation, because they have cast off their first faith. And withal they learn to be idle, wandering about from house to house; and not only idle, but tattlers also and busybodies, speaking things which they ought not. I will therefore that the younger women marry, bear children, guide the house, give none occasion to the adversary to speak reproachfully. For some are already turned aside after Satan.**
>
> **If any man or woman that believeth have widows, let them relieve them, and let not the church be charged; that it may relieve them that are widows indeed. Let the elders that rule well be counted worthy of double honour, especially they who labour in the word and doctrine. For the scripture saith, Thou shalt not muzzle the ox that treadeth out the corn. And, The labourer is worthy of his reward** (1 Timothy 5:9-18, paragraph breaks mine).

How Does a Woman Display Idleness?

In Chapter One, we identified one of the traits of the foolish woman as being destructive. Instead of using her hands to build up her home, she uses them to tear it down. Idleness accomplishes something similar: **by idleness of the hands the house will fall to pieces** (Ecclesiastes 10:18b LXX).

The way we understand the word "idleness" does not connote destructive activity so much as it indicates a lack of any activity at all. The Bible uses words like sloth and sluggard to describe such a person: **his hands do not choose to do anything** (Proverbs 21:25b LXX). However, what's interesting about doing nothing, from a Biblical standpoint, is that doing nothing is still considered a **work of thy hands** (Deuteronomy 16:15b LXX). In other words, doing nothing is a negative action, even though it is displayed by inaction. Similarly, a fence-sitter who believes that she is "safe" by showing no loyalty, is in effect, taking a negative position against both sides by being loyal to neither. Therefore, if an idle woman labours not at all, she is altogether unprofitable, like the **wicked and slothful servant** of Matthew 25:14-30. A slothful or unprofitable servant is like a **branch that beareth not fruit** (John 15:2) and will be taken away by the husbandman and cast **into the fire and they are burned** (John 15: 6).

In searching what the Bible had to say about idleness and unproductivity, I was led to discover that various labour and works that we perform can also be unproductive and unfruitful, and therefore relevant to this chapter.

There are two distinct kinds of work, or labour, as described in the Bible. The distinctions are illustrated in the following chart.

Labour in vain[3]	Labour in the Lord
Labour for the meat which perisheth[4]	Labour for the meat which endureth
Works of thy hands[5]	Works of God's hands

---

[3]   Ecclesiastes 2:17 LXX, "the work that was wrought under the sun was evil before me: for all is vanity and waywardness of spirit". "Under the sun" refers to "of the world". All such labour is vain. Labour that is for the Lord is all that which is committed unto Him, for His kingdom and glory. 1 Cor. 15:58, "your labour is not in vain in the Lord."

[4]   John 6:27, "Labour not for the meat which perisheth, but for the meat which endureth".

[5]   The Lord may "bless thee in all thy fruits, and in every work of thy hands" (Deut. 16:15 LXX); but, if all such works are performed "under the sun", or for your own glory, then you will find "vanity and waywardness of spirit" (Eccl. 2:11 LXX). The works of the hands that provoke God to wrath include serving strange gods or burning incense to them, acts of violence, and the worship of your own works (2 Kings 22:17 LXX, 2 Chron. 34:25 LXX, Is. 59:6 LXX, Jer.

Unprofitable[6]	Profitable
Wicked[7]	Righteous
Servant of sin unto death[8]	Servant of obedience unto righteousness

The first column contains futile, negative actions, while the second contains profitable and righteous actions. The first actions are derived from self-service and self-will, while the second are performed for the service and glory of the Lord. Adherence to the things of the first results in eternal death, while those of the second are rewarded with life everlasting. Every action we take, whether it be to do something or to do nothing, we take toward one of these two ends. Which column best describes the actions that you take?

With this overarching, dichotomous viewpoint in mind, the following topics will be discussed in this chapter: 1) the sluggard, 2) the vain labourer, 3) the unprofitable servant, and 4) the idle tattler.

1) The Sluggard.

Desires kill the sluggard; for his hands do not choose to do anything (Proverbs 21:25 LXX). A simple way to describe the sluggard is to say that she does little of what is useful. She is desirous to get gain and to accomplish something, but because she is idle, she does nothing but dream. **The sluggard says, I slumber a little, and I sleep a little, and for a little while I fold my arm across my breast. But if thou do this, thy poverty will come speedily; and thy want like a swift courier** (Proverbs 24:33, 34 LXX). Like a sailboat without wind to propel it forward, the sluggard

---

1:16, 25:6, 44:8 LXX, Acts 7:41, Rev. 9:20). The works of God's hands are all those things by reason of which we glorify God.

6   Exemplified by the unprofitable servant in Luke 17:10 and Matthew 25:30

7   Malachi 3:18 LXX, "Then shall ye return, and discern between the righteous and the wicked, and between him that serves God, and him that serves him not."

8   Romans 6:16, "Know ye not, that to whom ye yield yourselves servants to obey, his servants ye are to whom ye obey; whether of sin unto death, or of obedience unto righteousness?"; John 8:34, "Whosoever committeth sin is the servant of sin."

is fit for service, but does not set sail. **Every slothful man desires, but the hands of the active are diligent** (Proverbs 13:4 LXX). The Bible identifies two conditions that beset the sluggard: a) fear, and/or b) pride.

a) Fear

Fear casts down the slothful (Proverbs 18:8a LXX). When confronted with the obvious—the fact that she does not "get" because she does not "do"—**The sluggard makes excuses, and says, There is a lion in the ways, and murderers in the streets** (Proverbs 22:13 LXX). When the unprofitable servant of Matthew 25:14-30 was confronted for his laziness, his response was, **I was afraid** (Matthew 25:25a). The sluggard lacks the courage to do what needs to be done.

Fear tends to result from a lack of experience or knowledge. We are afraid of unforeseen, negative results. This presents us with a conundrum: we cannot be emboldened by positive results until we have overcome our fear consistently enough to experience them!

When I gave birth to my first child, I sustained an injury that left me unable to walk. For months, I could not leave the house unless my husband pushed me around in a wheelchair. Six months later, I had healed. Although I was able to get out of the house to run errands, I found myself in a state of fear-induced immobility. My legs worked, but my courage failed me! At first, it would take me three or four days to gather up enough courage to go outside. Then, it would take me a day, then a morning, until I finally got it down to a few hours. Without the help and strength of prayer, which made me visualize victory over my fear through the power of Christ, I would have remained fearful. The more I practised fearlessness, the more courageous I became.

The sluggard is similarly immobilized by fear. She knows what needs to be done, but is caught in a cycle of fear and doubt. God says, **Be strong, ye relaxed hands and palsied knees** (Isaiah 35:3 LXX). Action taken in the strength of the Lord is encouraging, lending itself to godly boldness and productive deeds. **Fear not; for I am with thee: wander not; for I am thy God, who have strengthened thee; and I have helped thee, and have established thee with my just right hand** (Isaiah 41:10 LXX).

b) Pride

Some idle women are proudly inactive rather than humbly serving. They foolishly believe that menial, domestic tasks are for the unintelligent, the oppressed, or the incompetent. This kind of **sluggard when reproached is not ashamed** (Proverbs 20:4a LXX). In Ezekiel 16, Sodom is accused of being prideful: **she and her daughters lived in pleasure, in fullness of bread and in abundance: this belonged to her and her daughters, and they helped not the hand of the poor and needy** (Ezekiel 16:49 LXX).[9] A proud and lazy woman looks haughtily at the hard-working, virtuous woman, thinking her common. She is too "classy" to get her hands dirty or wear an apron in service to others. **A sluggard seems to himself wiser than one who most satisfactorily brings back a message** (Proverbs 26:16 LXX). A woman like this takes pride in doing nothing.

The virtuous woman is the polar opposite of the sluggard. She **finds by experience that working is good; and her candle goes not out all night** (Proverbs 31:18 LXX). **She reaches forth her arms to needful works . . . she opens her hands to the needy, and reaches out fruit to the poor** (Proverbs 31:19a, 20 LXX). This woman, along with her entire household, is blessed: **She . . . rejoices in the last days** (Proverbs 31:25 LXX). Her husband is blessed: **The heart of her husband trusts in her** (Proverbs 31:11a LXX). He **is not anxious about those at home when he tarries anywhere abroad: for all her household are clothed** (Proverbs 31:21 LXX). He **becomes a distinguished person in the gates, when he sits in council with the old inhabitants of the land** (Proverbs 31:23 LXX). Her children are blessed: **And her kindness to them sets up her children for them, and they grow rich, and her husband praises her** (Proverbs 31:28 LXX). Ultimately, the virtuous, hard-working woman gains honour that exceeds that of any other: **Many daughters have obtained wealth, many have wrought valiantly; but thou hast exceeded, thou hast surpassed all** (Proverbs 31:29 LXX).

The wise and hard-working woman values what God values. She does not leave the keeping of her home or the training of her children to others. She takes on that responsibility for herself, knowing that her rewards will

---

[9]   Read James 5:1-6, Isaiah 10, Matthew 25:31-46, Job 24, and Amos 8 to learn what God thinks about those who fail to help the poor and needy.

come from her Father in heaven. A humble, hard-working woman knows that she has been **bought with a price** (1 Corinthians 6:20) and looks at service to others not only as a duty but as an opportunity to bless and be blessed.

> **For God is not unrighteous to forget your work and labour of love, which ye have shewed toward his name, in that ye have ministered to the saints, and do minister. And we desire that every one of you do shew the same diligence to the full assurance of hope unto the end: That ye be not slothful, but followers of them who through faith and patience inherit the promises** (Hebrews 6:10-12).

2) The Vain Labourer.

A picture of the vain labourer is painted clearly by King Solomon in the book of Ecclesiastes. His search is remarkable and his conclusion instructive. His research question is, **What advantage is there to a man in all his labour that he takes under the sun?** (Ecclesiastes 1:3 LXX). The labours performed under the sun are all those things that are **of the world** (1 John 2:16) or **under heaven** (Ecclesiastes 1:13 LXX). We all labour in one way or another, under the sun, every day. **All things are full of labour** (Ecclesiastes 1:8 LXX). Solomon applied all his heart to **seek out and examine by wisdom concerning all things** (Ecclesiastes 1:13 LXX) in order to see what advantage there was in any of it.

King Solomon tried it all. He tried laughter, wine, wealth, and abundance (Ecclesiastes 2:1-10 LXX). He examined the philosophies of men, from wisdom to foolishness (Ecclesiastes 2:12-16 LXX). He examined the times and seasons, the oppressed and the oppressor, the envied and the enviable (Ecclesiastes 3, 4 LXX). In the end, his conclusion was this: **I beheld all the works that were wrought under the sun; and, behold, all were vanity and waywardness of spirit** (Ecclesiastes 1:14 LXX). *All* were vanity. This means that everything we do apart from God is fruitless and vain. Sports, novels, movies, television shows, video games, shopping sprees, and most higher education are all worldly pursuits that indicate a wayward spirit.

Solomon's final advice is, **Fear God, and keep his commandments: for this is the whole man. For God will bring every work into judgment, with everything that has been overlooked, whether it be good, or whether it be evil** (Ecclesiastes 12:13, 14 LXX). We will be accountable for everything that we do, but only those things which are done in Christ will be profitable. **Be ye stedfast, unmoveable, always abounding in the work of the Lord, forasmuch as ye know that your labour is not in vain in the Lord** (1 Corinthians 15:58).

If all labour under the sun is vanity and indicative of a wayward spirit, and profitable labour is all that which we do for Christ, then our mission is clear. **Labour not for the meat which perisheth, but for the meat which endureth unto everlasting life, which the Son of man shall give unto you: for him hath God the Father sealed** (John 6:27).

Those who labour in the name of Christ manifest the **fruits of righteousness, which are by Jesus Christ, unto the glory and praise of God** (Philippians 1:11). Such fruit is observable. It is a witness of whom we serve.

For example, Anna, the prophetess we read about in Luke 2:36-38 was an aged widow whose self-discipline revealed her good service in Christ. She **departed not from the temple, but served God with fastings and prayers night and day** (Luke 2:37b). God rewarded her the same way He rewarded Simeon, a **just and devout** (Luke 2:25) man, by allowing them to gaze upon and bless the baby Jesus: **For mine eyes have seen thy salvation** (Luke 2:30), Simeon said of Jesus. Anna, **coming in that instant gave thanks likewise unto the Lord, and spake of him to all them that looked for redemption in Jerusalem** (Luke 2:38). They were recognized and rewarded for their devoted, disciplined service to the Most High God. Their labour was profitable.

3) The Unprofitable Servant.

A "Christian" who does not labour in Christ does not belong to Him. She is like the unprofitable servant, who is **cast into outer darkness** (Matthew 25:30a). In the parable of Matthew 25:14-30, three servants were given talents according to their abilities, or gifts. The first two received five and two talents, respectively, and used them faithfully in the service of their lord, and were rewarded. The third servant received only one talent, and instead of using it profitably, he buried it in the dirt. When confronted by his lord, he excused himself with the words, **I was afraid** (Matthew 25:25a). So is the idle woman. She receives the Word, and has the ability to share it with at least one other person, but is struck by fear, and rendered unprofitable. **For God hath not given us the spirit of fear; but of power, and of love, and of a sound mind** (2 Timothy 1:6b-7). When a proclaimed servant of God does not manifest her gifts in His name, she is like the wicked and slothful servant, and will be **cast into outer darkness** (Matthew 25:30).

Is it enough for us to serve God silently in our hearts, with all sincerity, and be justified? No. The Bible teaches us that belief alone in Christ is not enough. Faith must be accompanied by works: **What doth it profit, my brethren, though a man say he hath faith, and have not works? can faith save him?** (James 2:14). Our works must be manifest.

The sure way to be a profitable servant of the Most High God is to **Neglect not the gift that is in thee** (1 Timothy 4:14a). **As every man hath received the gift, even so minister the same one to another, as good stewards of the manifold grace of God** (1 Peter 4:10). A servant of God gives. When her gift is required, she gives it willingly as an act of service to her Eternal King. **For unto whomsoever much is given, of him shall be much required** (Luke 12:48).

Ye are not your own (1 Corinthians 6:19b), we are told. In everything we do, we yield ourselves in servitude to one of two masters. **Know ye not, that to whom ye yield yourselves servants to obey, his servants ye are to whom ye obey; whether of sin unto death, or of obedience unto righteousness?** (Romans 6:16). We have been **bought with a price: therefore glorify God in your body, and in your spirit, which are God's** (1 Corinthians 6:20). What a price God has paid for our souls! **I beseech you therefore, brethren, by the mercies of God, that ye present your bodies a living sacrifice, holy, acceptable unto God, which is your reasonable service** (Romans 12:1). Presenting ourselves to God as a vessel of service, ready and willing to do as He bids us, is our "reasonable service". It is not unreasonable, illogical, or unfair. It is proof of whom we serve; it is proof of our heavenly citizenship. **But love your enemies, and**

do good, and lend, hoping for nothing again; and your reward shall be great, and ye shall be children of the Highest (Luke 6:35a).

A profitable servant does the will of Christ, labouring as He did. **Verily, verily, I say unto you, He that believeth on me, the works that I do shall he do also** (John 14:12a). They bear fruit: **I have chosen you, and ordained you, that ye should go and bring forth fruit** (John 15:16a). Profitable labour is performed in the name of Christ and for the glory of God. Therefore, a "Christian" who does not use her gift profitably is not following Christ at all. Idleness is neither safe nor justified. It is an indication of whether we are alive in Christ, or dead in sin (Romans 6:11-13).

STUDY BREAK
Widows Indeed vs. The Younger Widows (1 Timothy 5:3, 11)

Reading 1st Timothy 5 as a new Christian perplexed me. I wondered how a young wife, after becoming widowed, would wax wanton against Christ and have damnation for casting off her first faith if she remarried. Usually, when I encountered difficulty with a passage, I would ask my husband what it meant and he would tell me. On this occasion, however, I took the advice that I had heard him tell countless others. He told people then the same thing he tells them today, "The Bible always interprets itself. If you seek an answer therein, you will find it". And so I sought. (Don't worry; I checked the results with him before writing them down!)

In order to unravel the meaning of 1 Timothy 5:12, we need to know what the Bible means by "first faith", "widowhood", and "marriage" as per the Biblical parallels God draws between Himself and the church. For this, we start in the Old Testament.

In their youth, the Israelites depended upon the Lord. They loved Him and were loyal to Him. They believed in Him. They made promises to Him (Jeremiah 2:1-2 LXX). As a result of their faith and obedience, God blessed and prospered them. However, after experiencing a life of plenty, they became distracted. They forgot their promises and what God did for them and forsook the **wife of thy youth** (Malachi 2:14).

A parallel is found in the New Testament book of Revelation. In chapter 2:4, the church of Ephesus was warned by Jesus to repent because, as He said to them, **thou hast left thy first love**. The young widows in 1 Timothy 5:12 **cast off their first faith**. These three concepts carry the same metaphor: the wife of their youth, their first love, and their first faith all refer to their faith in God.

The notion of "youth" repeated in these passages refers to the child-like trust that is unconditionally given to a parent or spouse. It is without guile, unsullied by the effects of worldly experience or godless living. It is given from a tender and vulnerable heart. The age, therefore, is not necessarily literal. You can be 64 and walk away from your "first faith".

Like those who grew up in a Christian home but later abandoned their beliefs, the Israelites forsook their faith in God: **the Lord has borne witness between thee and the wife of thy youth, whom thou has forsaken, and yet she was thy partner, and the wife of thy covenant** (Malachi 2:14 LXX). It is for this reason that when the Israelites forsook God, they were called a "harlot". They committed adultery against the Lord by going "a-whoring" after other gods (Ezekiel 16:35 LXX). This type of abandonment kindles God's wrath because it is akin to the betrayal of a once-beloved spouse. It is a covenant-breaker.

When the Israelites turned away from the wife of their youth and cast off their first faith, God treated them as adulterers and adulteresses. He departed from them and turned His face away from them. In keeping with marital parallels, the Bible describes this as being widowed by God.

The "widowhood" of the Israelites is defined in Isaiah 54 LXX. In verse 4, God promises them that they **shalt no more at all remember the reproach of thy widowhood**; in verses 7 and 8, widowhood is described in context: **For a little while I left thee**, and **in a little wrath I turned away my face from thee.** In Lamentations 1:1 LXX, Jeremiah describes the widowhood of Jerusalem, in that she is **made desolate . . . How does the city that was filled with people sit solitary! she is become as a widow** (Lamentations 1:1 LXX). This form of widowhood was a punishment for disloyalty. In the New Testament, 1 Peter 3:12 corroborates: **For the eyes of the Lord are over the righteous, and his ears are open unto their prayers: but the face of the Lord is against them that do evil.** 1st Timothy 5 follows through on this concept.

A "widow indeed" that Paul and Timothy refer to is defined as a woman who has lost her husband later in life and has subsequently devoted herself to God. She fasts, she prays, and she spends her days in the temple (1 Timothy 5:5). On the other hand, the young widow is like the Israelites who were taken care of by God; they were prospered and protected (Ezekiel 16:7-8 LXX). In the midst of their prosperity, they forgot God and went "a-whoring" after other gods.

The young widow whose husband has departed mourns for him. In her grief, she dedicates herself to the church, vowing to serve the Lord for the rest of her days. The church takes care of her and, over time, her mourning comes to an end. She prospers once again, forgets that she was desolate and in despair, and waxes **wanton against Christ** (1 Timothy 5:11b). In other words, she forgets the vow that she made to God when she was "young". This vow was her first love, or her first faith.

This is the same story as the Israelites who cast off their "first faith". They "married" other gods when they became disloyal to Christ. Their punishment was "widowhood", the turning away of God's face from them.

Paul says of the young widows, **for when they have begun to wax wanton against Christ, they will marry; Having damnation, because they have cast off their first faith** (1 Timothy 5:11b, 12). The young widow is lured away from her oath by the lusts of her flesh, and she becomes wanton for a man instead of remaining loyal to God. "Waxing wanton against Christ" is the same language as "going a-whoring after other gods".[10] In keeping with the parallel, 1 Timothy 5:12 says that the young widows "will marry" after they wax wanton against Christ. This, like adultery, is a covenant-breaker. This means that they will cease being loyal to God and give their loyalty away to another.

Let's look into this marriage concept a bit further. Two verses later, Paul says, **I will therefore that the younger women marry, bear children, guide the house** (1 Timothy 5:14). The young widow is not condemned because she wants to remarry; she is condemned because she has broken her vow not to remarry. Paul does not want a young widow to make a vow of celibacy that she cannot keep. With her witness as the Lord, who makes unbreakable vows, sealing believers forever with the promise of eternal life, she risks damnation if she fails to take her vows seriously.

---

[10]   Exodus 34:15-16, Leviticus 17:7, 20:5-6, Numbers 15:39, Deuteronomy 31:16, Judges 2:17, 8:27-33, 1 Chronicles 5:25, 2 Chronicles 21:13, Psalm 73:27, 106:39, Ezekiel 6:9, 23:30, Hosea 4:12, 9:1

In the Old Testament law, the husband of a woman who has made a vow can cancel it on her behalf (Numbers 30:8 LXX). A widow has no such recourse: **the vow of a widow and of her that is put away, whatsoever she shall bind upon her soul, shall stand to her** (Numbers 30:9 LXX). She is fully accountable before God for the vows she makes. Therefore Paul encourages her to remarry. Ultimately, her husband is her protection against making hasty promises that she cannot keep.

The young woman (less than 60 years old [1 Timothy 5:9]) who gets married, bears children, and guides the home after having been widowed (or "put away") is obeying the Word of God. She has a God-given opportunity to live a godly life under the spiritual protection of her new husband. She is commanded to serve him faithfully, to **give none occasion to the adversary to speak reproachfully** (1Timothy 5:14b). This is God's will for widowed or abandoned women.

4) The Idle Tattler.

When I imagine what a busybody looks like, I think of Lucille Ball. I imagine a silly woman who pries into matters that are not her own. She is more of a nuisance than a worker of iniquity. However, the busybody Paul speaks of in 1 Timothy 5 is not merely troublesome or meddlesome; she is **turned aside after Satan** (1 Timothy 5:15). This is no small matter.

The young widows are not at first idle. Paul says that they **learn to be idle, wandering about from house to house; and not only idle, but tattlers also and busybodies, speaking things which they ought not** (1 Timothy 5:13). The young widow starts to gossip, tell tales, and spread rumours.

Gossip is never harmless. It is deceitful and crafty, characterized by prejudice and misguided assumptions. **A faithful witness shall deliver a soul from evil: but a deceitful man kindles falsehoods** (Proverbs 14:25 LXX). Psalm 15 says that he who will dwell in God's holy mountain **has not spoken craftily with his tongue, neither has done evil to his neighbour, nor taken up a reproach against them** (Psalm 15:3 LXX). How often has it happened in your church that an offended party confides her hurt feelings to a friend and soon the entire church has vilified the purported offender? This is called "taking up a reproach" against someone. Matthew 18 gives us specific directions against such behaviour. Verse 15 says, **Moreover, if thy brother shall trespass against thee, go and tell him his fault between thee and him alone: if he shall hear thee, thou hast gained thy brother.**

The courageous, godly response to being offended by someone is to privately discuss the matter with the offender. Making the incident a matter for discussion with outside parties[11] is the mistake of the busybody. She is more concerned with dramatizing the event and causing a sensation in the church than she is with seeking a godly solution to a quietly resolvable problem. Not only does she exaggerate the severity of her own matters, but she also exaggerates matters that do not directly affect her. Her methods of interference are unrighteous and unholy.

Jesus said, **But I say unto you, that every idle word that men shall speak, they shall give an account thereof in the day of judgment** (Matthew 12:36). "Idle" words, the careless, meaningless ones we utter before we apply the appropriate filters inevitably come out and expose what lies in or hearts, for any discerning ear to hear. These words are what defile us. **Not that which goeth into the mouth defileth a man; but that which cometh out of the mouth, this defileth a man** (Matthew 15:11). A gossip is defiled by her tendency to speak carelessly and unproductively. **But let your communication be, Yea, yea; Nay, nay: for whatsoever is more than these cometh of evil** (Matthew 5:37). Productive, fruitful speech in Christ will **minister grace unto the hearers** (Ephesians 4:29b). This type of speech results from carefully considered, godly conversation.

For we hear that there are some which walk among you disorderly, working not at all, but are busybodies (2 Thessalonians 3:11). In this passage, Paul is referring to church workers who fail to work for their food. They are idle. In their free time, they sit around and talk. Idle conversation tends to digress, going off-topic, into crooked tangents which Paul calls **disorder**, also known as **perverse disputings** (1 Timothy 6:5). Paul writes, **study to be quiet, and to do your own business** (1 Thessalonians 4:11a). **Neither give heed to fables and endless geneaologies, which minster questions, rather than godly edifying which is in faith** (1 Timothy 1:4).

---

[11]   Please read Matthew 18:16-17 to learn what to do if the private discussion proves fruitless.

The young widow, in her capacity as a tale-bearer, is in danger of spreading false doctrine. **And they shall turn away their ears from the truth, and shall be turned unto fables** (2 Timothy 4:4). Today, this occurs through the simple act of reading a "Christian" book that contains false doctrine, and then telling someone what it says. Just like the Athenians who **spent their time in nothing else, but either to tell, or to hear some new thing** (Acts 17:21), the busybody just can't wait to tell someone what she has heard or read. **Beware lest any man spoil you through philosophy and vain deceit, after the tradition of men, after the rudiments of the world, and not after Christ** (Colossians 2:8). If it has itched her ears (stroked her ego), she will spread it as truth. Her vanity will dissolve her critical filter, not allowing her to **endure sound doctrine** (2 Timothy 4:3). She will become convinced of a false doctrine.

The idle tattler wanders off one day to visit a friend and tells the friend what she heard. The friend finds that it tickles her ears, too. She tells another friend and the false story spreads like a disease, and it infects the entire church. People lose their way and lose their faith. All this occurs because of the careless actions of a silly, senseless woman. She has graduated from being a mere nuisance to becoming a real worker of iniquity. **Thou wilt destroy all that speak falsehood** (Psalm 5:6a LXX).

Modern Snapshot
SUSAN

Susan was married to a stalwart, Christian man. They had three wonderful children and a happy home. They were exemplary members of the community, involved in several philanthropic societies and outreach programs. When she was fifty and he was fifty-four, he died.

As a young widow, she remained a respectable member of the community. She continued to be a regular member of the church. Life went on. Her children, however, lost their way. One became a drug addict and never settled down. The other married a drunkard and got divorced. The third went off to travel the world and remained elsewhere. Susan was left alone in a big house with little to do.

The social life of the church soon revolved around Susan. She made the announcements every Sunday morning at church. She organized church dinners, outings, and camps. She was bright, friendly, and sociable. She soon became involved in church politics. She was on several committees and was making decisions that affected the entire church. If a decision did not go her way, she would make sure that it did.

By speaking craftily, Susan became highly influential and maintained high social status in the church. She spread selective rumours, coming to the "aid" of offended parties. By being the confidante of other women in the church, she was able to take up reproaches on their behalf, effectively playing the virtuous heroine whose "compassion" and "justice" kept church members in line.

One day, while making the Sunday morning announcements, something slipped. During her morning prayer, she referred to God as "her". Not a single man in the 200-person congregation raised his voice in protest. When a woman asked her about it following the service, Susan explained to the woman exactly why she thought God was female. In a book she had read, she learned that God must possess female attributes in order to create woman. (That would be like saying that God must be part rock in order to create rock.)

Susan's friend liked the sound of God being a she. In fact, thinking of God as a female made her feel "closer" to Him, more familiar, and more special. It elevated her ego and tickled her ears. A few months later, one third of the women in the church had read that book, followed Susan's example, and had begun to refer to God as a woman. Again, not a single member of the congregation raised his or her voice in protest. They watched idly while a third of the church members became idol worshippers. Susan and her friends left their *first faith*, and *turned aside after Satan*. They have earned for themselves *damnation*.

Today, that church still exists. Its membership count has decreased by two thirds. A few of the faithful remain along with the idol-worshipping women who bring their brow-beaten husbands to church with them. Susan and her friends have recently hired a new preacher who happens to be a woman. She teaches that the apostle Peter was a misogynist, a woman-hater. She, too, has turned aside after Satan and it is only a matter of time before the entire church becomes apostate.

This is why God hates liars. He hates the cowards who fail to stand up for the truth and He hates the deceivers that lead astray the sheep. He is a just God.

> **But the fearful, and unbelieving, and the abominable,**
> **and murderers, and whoremongers, and sorcerers,**
> **and idolaters, and all liars, shall have their part**
> **in the lake which burneth with fire and brimstone:**
> **which is the second death** (Revelation 21:8).

Summary

A sluggard is immobilized by fear and/or pride. She has a strong desire to accomplish much, but lacks the courage and/or humility to do so. The vain labourer accomplishes much, but her labours are worldly, and therefore lack eternal value. An unprofitable servant has received the gospel message and been compelled by it, but is too fearful to share it with others. She has been gifted for this purpose, but lays waste her gifts. Finally, an idle tattler speaks carelessly or craftily of serious matters. She spreads falsehoods and causes others to lose their way and potentially, their faith as well.

A virtuous woman, on the other hand, is a labourer "worthy of her hire". She labours for the meat that endures. She labours in the Truth, in the Word, and in sound doctrine (1 Timothy 4:6). She is profitable because she uses her gifts to bless and to edify her husband, her children, and the needy. She is neither lazy nor idle. Her gratitude toward God for granting her the gift of salvation is never forgotten in her pursuit to lead a godly life. It motivates her to present herself to God as **a living sacrifice, holy, acceptable unto God** (Romans 12:1). She does so for His glory, knowing that it is her reasonable service to do so. She will arise and do, for the Lord is with her. **And I heard a voice from heaven saying unto me, Write, Blessed are the dead which die in the Lord from henceforth: Yea, saith the Spirit, that they may rest from their labours; and their works do follow them** (Revelation 14:13).

Who Shall Deliver Me?

- **And, behold, I come quickly; and my reward is with me, to give every man according as his work shall be** (Revelation 22:12).
- **In a little wrath I turned away my face from thee; but with everlasting mercy will I have compassion upon thee, saith the Lord that delivers thee** (Isaiah 54:8 LXX).
- **And the Lord shall deliver me from every evil work, and will preserve me unto his heavenly kingdom: to whom be glory for ever and ever. Amen** (2 Timothy 4:18).
- **And you, that were sometime alienated and enemies in your mind by wicked works, yet now hath he reconciled In the body of his flesh through death, to present you holy and unblameable and unreproveable in his sight: If ye continue in the faith grounded and settled, and be not moved away from the hope of the gospel** (Colossians 1:21-23a).
- **For we are [God's] workmanship, created in Christ Jesus unto good works, which God hath before ordained that we should walk in them** (Ephesians 2:10).

How Can I Be Fruitful?

- Labour in the gospel (Philippians 4:3).
- Labour in prayers (Colossians 4:12).
- Labour to enter into rest (Hebrews 4:11).
- Be a burden to no one (2 Corinthians 12:14).
- Be diligent (2 Peter 3:15).
- Be sober (Titus 2:4).
- Be vigilant (1 Peter 5:8).
- Bear much fruit (John 15:8).
- Do the will of God (Mathew 7:21).
- Obey them that have the rule over you (Hebrews 13:17).
- Esteem others higher than yourself (Philippians 2:3).
- Love one another (John 13:34).
- Follow after charity (1 Corinthians 14:1).

- Serve one another (Galatians 5:13).
- Know them which labour among you and esteem them highly in love (1 Thessalonians 5:12, 13).
- Give the light of the knowledge of the glory of God (2 Corinthians 4:6).
- Bless them that curse you (Luke 6:28).
- Pray for them that despitefully use you (Luke 6:28).
- Avenge not yourselves (Romans 12:19).
- Give God the praise (John 9:24).
- Give alms (Luke 11:41).
- Give thanks (1 Thessalonians 5:18).
- Give an answer to every man that asketh you a reason of the hope that is in you (1 Peter 3:15).
- Live peaceably with all men (Romans 12:18).
- Give none offence (1 Corinthians 10:32).
- Be given to hospitality (1 Peter 4:9).
- Give diligence to make your calling and election sure (2 Peter 1:10).
- Give none occasion to the adversary to speak reproachfully (1 Timothy 5:14).
- Give heed to what you hear from the Lord (Hebrews 2:1).
- Walk in the Spirit (Galatians 5:16).
- Be good stewards of the manifold grace of God (1 Peter 4:10).
- Attend upon the Lord without distraction (1 Corinthians 7:35).
- Overcome evil with good (Romans 12:21).

Think on These Things

1. Do I look at my work as a blessing?
   Deut. 16:15
2. Do I seek monetary rewards rather than spiritual ones?
   Luke 6:35
3. Does God judge me for what I don't do?
   Mat. 25:41-46

4. How are we considered righteous?

   Mat. 25:34-40

5. Why am I to serve?

   1 Cor. 6:20

6. Doesn't my salvation guarantee me a place in heaven no matter what I do?

   1 Cor. 3:15

7. How can I serve God?

   Rom. 12:1

8. What kind of works does God expect of me?

   John 14:2

9. Isn't faith enough?

   James 2:14-26

10. How does what I do affect others?

    Mat. 5:16

11. What are the spiritual rewards we receive from our faithfulness?

    Mat. 25:23

12. What do I do when I feel overworked?

    Is. 43:1-7, Mat. 11:28-30

CHAPTER SIX

TO USURP AUTHORITY
1 TIMOTHY 2:12

Profile #6: The Usurper
Be Under Obedience (1 Corinthians 14:34)
EVE

E ve was created by God to be a **help suitable to** Adam (Genesis 2:18 LXX). She was a unique being, made as the same kind as Adam, but not in the same image as Adam. She is distinctly female. The man is **the image and glory of God: but the woman is the glory of the man** (1 Corinthians 11:7b). She is the only living being created by God from another living being. As such, she is incredibly special.

God created a garden for Adam to live in prior to the creation of Eve. Adam was given specific instructions by God to **cultivate and keep it. And the Lord God gave a charge to Adam, saying, Of every tree which is in the garden thou mayest freely eat, but of the tree of the knowledge of good and evil—of it ye shall not eat, but in whatsoever day ye eat of it, ye shall surely die** (Genesis 2:15b-17 LXX).

God said, **It is not good that the man should be alone** (Genesis 2:18 LXX). God created and brought each kind of creature before Adam **to see what he would call them** (Genesis 2:19 LXX). Adam named them all, but **there was not found a help like to himself** (Genesis 2:20 LXX). So God made Eve and brought her to Adam. Adam said, **This now is bone of my bones, and flesh of my flesh; she shall be called woman, because she was taken out of her husband** (Genesis 2:23 LXX).

Adam and Eve lived in obedience to the Lord. However, soon Eve's willingness to obey God's commandment would be tested. **The serpent was the most crafty of all the brutes on the earth, which the Lord God made, and the serpent said to the woman, Wherefore has God said, Eat not of every tree of the garden?**

> **And the woman said to the serpent, We may eat of the fruit of the trees of the garden, but of the fruit of the tree which is in the midst of the garden, God said, Ye shall not eat of it, neither shall ye touch it, lest ye die.**
>
> **And the serpent said to the woman, Ye shall not surely die. For God knew that in whatever day ye should eat of it your eyes would be opened, and ye would be as gods, knowing good and evil.**
>
> **And the woman saw that the tree was good for food, and that it was pleasant to the eyes to look upon and beautiful to contemplate, and having taken of its fruit she ate, and she gave to her husband also with her, and they ate** (Genesis 3:1-6 LXX, paragraph breaks mine).

In that day they were no longer immortal, but doomed to die; **by one man's offence death reigned** (Romans 5:17a). God said to Eve, **I will greatly multiply thy pains and thy groanings; in pain thou shalt bring forth children, and thy submission shall be to thy husband, and he shall rule over thee** (Genesis 3:16 LXX).

STUDY BREAK
Pulling Down Strongholds (2 Corinthians 10:4)

Paul tells us that **the weapons of our warfare are not carnal, but mighty through God to the pulling down of strongholds** (2 Corinthians 10:4). His point is that while we cannot rely on our own power (the power of the flesh) to defeat satanic philosophies, we can rely on God's power (the power of the Spirit). Satanic philosophies are defined in the next verse: **every high thing that exalteth itself against the knowledge of God** (2 Corinthians 10:5). Knowledge that is anti-Christ is satanic. Before we continue this chapter, there are three such philosophies that must be pulled down.

The first thing we need to fully establish in this chapter is the inerrancy of scripture: **For all the words of God are tried in the fire** (Proverbs 30:5a LXX).[1] This means that all of God's words are pure, eternal, and indestructible. Many of those who stand in defiance of God's words to women claim that the men who penned them leaked their biased, misogynist views into scripture. Some believe that the verses pertaining to women are culture-bound or specific only to a certain period of time. Others call such verses uninspired. Still others think that because woman's social status has changed, the rules should also change. While many of these beliefs are popular, none of them are true, and none of them justify disobedience to the Word of God. Jesus said to the greedy, power-hungry Pharisees, **Ye are they which justify yourselves before men; but God knoweth your hearts: for that which is highly esteemed among men is abomination in the sight of God** (Luke 16:15).

We are assured that **no prophecy[2] of the scripture is of any private interpretation[3]** (2 Peter 1:20). This means that the scripture is inspired by God, and not written as a man might write it. Bias is common in works that are written by men; however, the Bible is the only book in the world that is God-breathed, and therefore flawless. **All scripture[4] is given by inspiration of God** (2 Timothy 3:16a). God did not use just anyone to write His Word; **holy men of God spake as they were moved by the Holy Ghost** (2 Peter 1:21b). Paul rejoiced over the church at Thessalonica for their faith and belief in God **because, when ye received the word of God which ye heard of us, ye received it not as the word of men, but as it is in truth, the word of God, which effectually worketh also**

---

[1] See also 2 Samuel 22:31 LXX

[2] Prophecy is speech that is inspired by the Holy Ghost. It is a spiritual gift that both men and women can receive. See Romans 12:6, 1 Cor. 12:10, Revelation 19:10. "Prophecy of scripture" are the words written by men who were inspired by the Holy Spirit.

[3] i.e., bias

[4] By "scripture", please recognize that we are talking about the *inspired* Word of God, not the satanic counterfeit "Bibles" that are becoming common in the world today.

in you that believe (1 Thessalonians 2:13). Only gross arrogance and a truly wayward spirit would provoke any so-called Christian to deny this rudimentary fact.

God is as invariable as His Word. His word **abides in heaven forever** (Psalm 119:89b LXX). His truth **endures to all generations** (Psalm 119:90a LXX). His words have not, nor will not, ever fall to the ground,[5] be disproven, or out-dated. If we do not believe this to be true, then we are denying the omnipotence of God and have no business calling ourselves the followers of Christ.

The second point to acknowledge in this chapter is the fact of our servitude. We tend to recoil when we hear the words servant, slavery, or subservience. If we are followers of Christ, we are His servants. We have been bought with a price, and are therefore His "slaves". There is no shame in that. In fact, without the free-will offering of our body, soul, and spirit as a sacrifice to the Living God, who owns us, there is neither gain nor glory, there is neither heaven nor eternal life, there is neither justification nor regeneration. Jesus told His disciples, **If any man will come after me, let him deny himself, and take up his cross, and follow me** (Matthew 16:24). It is of primary importance that we deny our ego, which is our Self, in order to exercise servitude to the will of God, who became our Lord and Master on the day we chose to believe on Him.

Jesus Christ **made himself of no reputation, and took upon him the form of a servant . . . he humbled himself, and became obedient unto death, even the death of the cross** (Philippians 2:7-8). This is the mind of Christ, which we are to share. Our subservience to our husbands is a direct reflection of our subservience to Christ (Ephesians 5:24, 25). If we bend our will to Christ, as dutiful "slaves", appreciating the honour due our benevolent Master, then bending our will to our husbands in similar fashion is a small matter, one which is performed readily, with ease, gladness, and hope.

---

5   This phrase appears in relation to the fulfillment of prophecies made by OT prophets. The words that come true are those which are upheld or kept, "gone abroad", as opposed to those which fall meaninglessly away, having been proven false. For example, 1 Samuel 3:19 LXX says, "And Samuel grew, and the Lord was with him, and there did not fall one of his words to the ground". In other words, all of his prophecies were fulfilled.

On the night of His betrayal, Jesus removed his coat, tied his robe into pants, fastened a towel to his waist, poured water into a basin, and stooped down to wash the disciples' feet (John 13:4-5). Such a subservient act was considered loathsome to the Jews. Similar, in fact, to the way today's culture views subservient women who wait on their husbands "hand and foot". After humbling Himself in this manner, Jesus said to the disciples:

> **Ye call me Master and Lord: and ye say well; for so I am. If I then, your Lord and Master, have washed your feet; ye also ought to wash one another's feet. For I have given you an example, that ye should do as I have done to you. Verily, verily, I say unto you, The servant is not greater than his lord; neither he that is sent greater than he that sent him. If ye know these things, happy are ye if ye do them** (John 13:13-17).

By removing our pride, humbling ourselves into servants, and taking on the appropriate tools and attire, we ensure for ourselves the rewards of the profitable servant, who was told, **Well done, thou good and faithful servant: thou hast been faithful over a few things, I will make thee ruler over many things: enter thou into the joy of thy lord** (Matthew 25:21). As willing servants, our glory on this earth will be minimal, and while we may suffer persecution, mockery, and contempt, our rewards in heaven will be great, and our crown of jewels will sparkle brightest. The meekness and lowliness of heart exemplified by Christ is never to be disdained by those who would follow Him into the realms of His heavenly kingdom.

The third thing to be acknowledged in this chapter is that God gives us commandments to bless us. **For this is the love of God, that we keep his commandments: and his commandments are not grievous** (1 John 5:3). Often, when we are given rules, we consider them inconvenient or oppressive because we fail to see the safeguards that are built therein. For example, we teach our children to play outside on the lawn, but they are not to go on the road. We do not give them this restriction to hinder their freedom or to oppress them; we give it to them for their safety. So it is with God's Word. God's restrictions pertaining to women are for our blessing and safety. They benefit us, our marriage, and the entire church body. This chapter will reveal those blessings to you, so that you may know, understand, and appreciate them. **O that there were such a heart in them, that they should fear me and keep my commands always, that it might be well with them and with their sons for ever** (Deuteronomy 5:29 LXX).

King David said to the Lord, **Thine ordinances**[6] **were my songs in the place of my sojourning** (Psalm 119:54 LXX). It is my hope that you will be singing these songs by the end of the chapter!

How Does A Woman Usurp Authority?

A usurper seizes or assumes power wrongfully.[7] Her motivation is greed, or avarice, which is a strong, selfish desire for money, gain, or control. An avaricious woman wrongfully seizes the authority that God has appointed to men, or more specifically, to her husband. This is a simple matter of appointment. Those who complicate this matter speak conveniently of equality, tolerance, compassion, or modernity. They are all missing the point, which is that **all members have not the same office** (Romans 12:4b). This office is established by God; to defy it is to sin against Him (Romans 13:2).

Women **are commanded to be under obedience, as also saith the law** (1 Corinthians 14:34b). What does the Bible say, directly from the mouth of the Lord regarding women? **Thy submission shall be to thy husband, and he shall rule over thee** (Genesis 3:16b LXX).

Our God is a God of order: **For Adam was first formed, then Eve** (1 Timothy 2:13). In the Garden of Eden, He established order by creating Adam first, then setting him over **all things** (Psalm 8:6 LXX). Adam was charged to "cultivate and keep" the garden, and to name all the creatures that God had made. When God saw that Adam was alone, He created for him a helper.

That helper is woman, and when a woman attempts to jump rank by becoming the leader, she is disobeying a direct order from God. **But I suffer not a woman to teach, nor to usurp authority over the man,**

---

[6]   God's ordinances are rules or commands.

[7]   *The Oxford English Reference Dictionary*

but to be in silence (1 Timothy 2:12). If she usurps man's authority, as ordained by God for the church, she is failing to follow the chain of command that God has established, and like Eve, she will bear the consequences of her sin.

The serpent tempted Eve the same way that he tempts you and me every day. He was successful then and he is successful now for the same reasons. This chapter will discuss those reasons, so that we can learn from them. Keep in mind that the devil is a liar: **for he is a liar, and the father of it** (John 8:44b). We can see the manner by which he beguiled Eve in the following ways: 1) he sought the weak link, and 2) he sabotaged the chain of command. The third part of this chapter will discuss 3) God's safeguards for women.

1) He sought the weak link.

While most women (not all) can readily confess that they are physically weaker than men, few learn to embrace the reality of another weakness. Eve's story reveals it. Women are more likely to be deceived than men: **And Adam was not deceived, but the woman being deceived was in the transgression** (1 Timothy 2:14).

I distinctly remember the day I read this as a new Christian. I felt the heat of shame rise in my cheeks, and I was stricken. I did not want to share the blame for Eve's fall. However, the issue was not blame. The issue was truth, and the Bible is true. I had to change the way I thought. Despite what I wanted to believe, I had to come to terms with the fact that I was more susceptible to deception than the devil would have me believe.

Confronting this susceptibility to deception are two stories that the Bible provides for us to learn by: a) Dinah, the daughter of Jacob, and b) the elect lady of 2 John.

a) Dinah

Dinah was the only daughter born to Jacob. Genesis 34 tells us her brief but tragic story. After leaving his brother, Esau, on good terms, Jacob took his family and settled in the land of Canaan, by the city of Shechem.

Dinah **went forth to observe the daughters of the inhabitants** (Genesis 34:1 LXX). This is such an informative verse. It tells us a few things about Dinah.

First, it tells us that she was curious. If she had just come from visiting Esau, she would have known that Esau unwisely intermarried with Canaanite women. She would have known that the Canaanites were a godless people. Nevertheless, she decided to go out to "observe" them.

This type of curiosity is similar to the desire to gawk at road kill, or to "rubber-neck" at a car collision on the freeway. All Dinah would see were the walking dead: women who lived in pleasure (1 Timothy 5:6). By observing godlessness, those who are fascinated by it allow themselves to experience it vicariously. Does this sound familiar? Young "Christian" girls do this in our society every weekend if they go into a godless city to see and be seen and they do it if they turn their eyes toward a secular movie or television show. They think that their "curiosity" justifies them, and so do their unwise parents. **Go not in the ways of the ungodly, neither covet the ways of transgressors. In whatever place they shall pitch their camp, go not thither; but turn from them, and pass away** (Proverbs 4:14-15 LXX).

The second thing we learn about Dinah is that she went without the protection of either her father or her brothers. Dinah was a young, beautiful Hebrew woman embarking on a sightseeing journey into a godless city. She had no one to keep her safe, to defend her honour, or to protect her from evil. She foolishly relied on herself.

What was the result of Dinah and her mother's unwariness?[8] **And [Shechem] the son of [Hamor the Hivite], the ruler of the land, saw her, and took her and lay with her, and humbled her** (Genesis 34:2 LXX). Although Dinah may have been accompanied by women, including her mother Leah, not one of those women had the ability to keep her from being kidnapped by Shechem's men and subsequently violated by Shechem.[9] Any one of her brothers could have prevented this tragedy if they had been there.[10]

---

[8] The full account can be found in the book of Jasher, chapter 33.

[9] This detail is given in the book of Jasher, chapter 33.

[10] Simeon and Levi slew every man of Shechem when they later went to liberate Dinah. According to the book of Jasher, the sons of Jacob were mighty men who

b) The elect lady

2 John is written to **the elect lady and her children** (2 John 1). We do not know exactly who the elect lady is in relation to John or the church, but we do know this about her: she is elect, which means that she is a member of the body of Christ.[11]

John tells her that **many deceivers are entered into the world, who confess not that Jesus Christ is come in the flesh. This is a deceiver and an antichrist** (2 John 7). Because the church is beset by deceivers who prey upon unprotected women, John understands the necessity of providing a timely warning. He offers her specific instructions pertaining to her conduct towards a deceiver. To safeguard herself from his influence, he advises her: **If there come any unto you, and bring not this doctrine, receive him not into your house, neither bid him God speed: For he that biddeth him God speed is partaker of his evil deeds** (2 John 10-11).

From this passage, we learn that a woman is not to give any opportunity to a false teacher to influence her. She may not invite him into her home or treat him as a member of the church. She is to turn him away. This is not an act of inhospitality; it is an act towards the preservation of the soul. **He that receives instruction shall be in prosperity; and he that regards reproofs shall be made wise. He that keeps his ways, preserves his own soul** (Proverbs 16:17b LXX).

See then that ye walk circumspectly, not as fools, but as wise (Ephesians 5:15). A woman who fails to turn away purveyors of false doctrine assumes that she can withstand their influence by her own power. By being unwise, she risks losing **those things which we have wrought** (2 John 8). Those things are the doctrine of salvation and the truth of Christ. Paul also says **continue thou in the things which thou hast learned** (2 Timothy 3:14).

Women are negligent when they fail to take necessary precautions. If they allow deceivers into their homes, or have become friends with the world, and have resisted the authorities that God has put in place for their protection, they are in danger of being led away from the truth of Christ. **But I fear, lest by any means, as the serpent beguiled Eve through his**

---

had exceptional physical strength, explaining how such a seemingly impossible feat happened.

[11] Mark 13:27, Luke 18:7, Romans 8:33

subtilty, so your minds should be corrupted from the simplicity that is in Christ (2 Corinthians 11:3).

Peter likens Satan to a lion on the prowl. Lions target the weakest prey. They give chase, separating the weak animals from the rest of the herd. Once their prey has been isolated, they chase it down for the kill. Then they devour it. **Be sober, be vigilant; because your adversary the devil, as a roaring lion, walketh about, seeking whom he may devour** (1 Peter 5:8). This verse precisely reveals the manner by which Satan works. Women are the weaker vessel, and they are his most vulnerable target.

The elect lady in 2 John is told to turn away the deceiver without showing him any special hospitality. If she helps him, she is **partaker of his evil deeds** (2 John 11). Feel the gravity of that statement. If you do not turn away the false doctrines of the world and put them out of your house, you are a partaker of Satan's evil deeds. While the elect lady had to turn away a person who represented false teachings, in our day we have to turn away the television or the computer. Protect yourself, and protect your children! Chances are that your husband is less prone to deception than you are. Encourage and allow him to do the discerning for you.[12]

For the husband is the head of the wife, even as Christ is the head of the church: and he is the saviour of the body (Ephesians 5:23). Husbands are uniquely qualified and appointed by God to rule over us (Genesis 3:16 LXX). They are to love us (Colossians 3:19) and to keep us safe (Ephesians 5:29). They receive and teach the Word to us,[13] they account and watch for our souls,[14] and they intercede on our behalf.[15]

The usurping woman does not allow her husband to fulfill these God-given roles for her. Like Dinah or her mother, she will leave the protection of her husband, father or older brother, uttering the prideful cry, "I can take care of *myself*!" Such folly precedes destruction (Proverbs 16:18 LXX). Hannah, the mother of Samuel, said, **Boast not, and utter not high things; let not high-sounding words come out of your mouth** (1 Samuel 2:3 LXX).

---

[12] If your husband is falling short in this area, my husband recommends Stephen and Alex Kendrick, *The Resolution for Men* (Nashville, TN: B&H Publishing Group, 2011).

[13] 1 Corinthians 14:35-36, Hebrews 13:7, 1 Thessalonians 5:12, 13

[14] 1st Timothy 3:4, 5, 12; Ephesians 5:23, Hebrews 13:17.

[15] Genesis 25:21 LXX, 1 Peter 3:7

Jerusalem was guilty of the same thing when she resisted the loving protection of her heavenly Father: **O Jerusalem, Jerusalem, thou that killeth the prophets, and stoneth them which are sent unto thee, how often would I have gathered thy children together, even as a hen gathereth her chickens under her wings, and ye would not!** (Matthew 23:37). God's discerning protection is similar to our husband's. It is no shame to accept it. It is an act of humility and grace.

The most powerful women are those who submit to the will of God. They accept the fact that they are easier to deceive than men. Their power rests in their reliance on God, and if applicable, their father or husband. **For when I am weak, then am I strong** (2 Corinthians 12:10b). Those who say that they will not or cannot be deceived have proven themselves to have been deceived already.

Satan, as the serpent, was both crafty and subtle. He knew that Adam would be more resistant to his influence, so he approached the "weaker vessel" when her protector was not nearby.[16] Instead of walking away and refusing to speak to him without her husband present, Eve remained and listened to his carefully crafted words. She denied herself the God-given protection of her husband and functioned unilaterally. She went out from under Adam's authority. As a result, she was deceived.

2) The Chain of Command.

Let all things be done decently and in order (1 Corinthians 14:40). In the absence of order, there is lawlessness and iniquity. **Order my steps according to thy word: and let not any iniquity have dominion over**

---

[16] Genesis 3:6b LXX states that after Eve contemplated the idea of eating the fruit, "having taken of its fruit she ate, and she gave to her husband also with her, and they ate". (Please note the use of the past participle for her action, but the simple past for his). It was in Genesis 3:1 (5 verses earlier) that the serpent approached Eve. If Adam was present at that point, Satan would have had to approach "them", which he did not. The serpent spoke "to the woman" (vs. 1b). His craftiness (he was "the most crafty of all the brutes..." vs. 1a) is illustrated by the fact that he approached Eve singularly. There is NO indication in the text that Adam was present at that time, or that he idly stood by as the serpent duped her, instead that after eating it, Eve went to Adam and then they ate it together.

me (Psalm 119:133 LXX). Our God is a God of order. He has ordered creation. The home is ordered; the church is ordered. The return of Jesus Christ is ordered. To defy God's order is to defy His very will and to sin against Him. Such sin invariably brings about reproach. **Whosoever therefore resisteth the power, resisteth the ordinance of God: and they that resist shall receive to themselves damnation** (Romans 13:2).

After Paul warns the woman not to usurp authority over the man in 1st Timothy 2:12, he gives the following justification: **For Adam was first formed, then Eve** (1 Timothy 2:13). Not only was order established in the six days of creation based on what was formed first and last, but also order was established with times, seasons, days, and weeks. To further substantiate the importance of order, the books of the law convince us of how significant it is to follow God's precise timing in carrying out His instructions. The accurate fulfillment of prophecy depends upon it.

For example, firstborn sons are considered holy unto the Lord: **Every male that openeth the womb shall be called holy to the Lord** (Luke 2:23). Throughout the law, the Israelites were told to give God the firstfruits of their labours. As sacrifices, they were to be the firstborn, or the firstfruits.[17] This is significant because Jesus, God's "firstborn" Son, fulfilled the requirements of the Old Testament law by His death on the cross. He personified the unflawed, innocent firstborn lamb that was sacrificed on the night of the Passover. Only its blood would suffice. The order that is established by God is therefore perfected and proven in the fulfillment of Jesus Christ. Without the proper order, the fulfillment of prophecy is nullified. Jesus said, **Think not that I am come to destroy the law, or the prophets: but to fulfill** (Matthew 6:17).

The first man Adam was made a living soul; the last Adam was made a quickening spirit (1 Corinthians 15:45). Jesus was the last Adam and has "become the firstfruits" (1 Corinthians 15:47, 20). He was the first to rise from the dead, so that we can all rise from the dead. **For as in Adam all die, even so in Christ shall all be made alive** (1 Corinthians 15:22). This parallel is not to be taken lightly. It is an indication of God's holy and established order. **But every man in his own order:**

---

17 The firstfruits of our labours, in the Old Testament, include the first harvest of crops (fruit, wheat, etc.), as well as the firstborn lamb, goat, calf, etc., to be offered as a sacrifice unto the Lord.

Christ the firstfruits; afterward they that are Christ's at his coming (1 Corinthians 15:23).

Until He comes, we are commanded by God to obey those who have been appointed to rule over us in Christ. This is how order is maintained. **Obey them that have the rule over you, and submit yourselves: for they watch for your souls as they that must give account, that they may do it with joy, and not with grief: for that is unprofitable for you** (Hebrews 13:17). By refusing to submit to her husband, a usurping wife places a burden on her husband heavy to be borne. Her resistance to God's order brings grief upon them both. Like Saul on the road to Damascus, persecuting the Lord, ignorant of the glorious freedom that comes from submission to Him, **it is hard for thee to kick against the pricks** (Acts 9:5b).[18] It is altogether unprofitable.

Paul tells us that the man is the **image and glory of God: but the woman is the glory of the man** (1 Corinthians 11:7b). A king is not glorified unless he has subordinates who bend the knee to him. God is not glorified unless man subordinates himself to Him. Neither does a wife give her husband glory unless she subjects herself to her husband. Remember, wives are told to submit to their **own husbands as unto the Lord** (Ephesians 5:22). Therefore, a husband/wife relationship does not accurately represent Christ's relationship to the church unless she gives her husband glory by subordinating herself to him. **Therefore as the church is subject unto Christ, so let the wives be to their own husbands in every thing** (Ephesians 5:24). Her lawful subjection to her husband is a completion of God's holy and ordained command structure.

And the woman said to the serpent, We may eat of the fruit of the trees of the garden, but of the fruit of the tree which is in the midst of the garden, God said, Ye shall not eat of it, neither shall ye touch it, lest ye die (Genesis 3:2-3 LXX). Eve knew the commandment of the Lord. She recited it perfectly to the serpent.

And the serpent said to the woman, Ye shall not surely die. For God knew that in whatever day ye should eat of it your eyes would

---

[18] The "pricks" refer to a goad, or prod that rested behind working oxen. If the oxen stubbornly refused to walk forward, but resisted their commands and stepped backward, they would injure themselves against the goad. Similarly, those who stubbornly resist God's instruction bring injury upon themselves.

be opened, and ye would be as gods, knowing good and evil (Genesis 3:4-5 LXX). The serpent told Eve a blatant lie and she fell for it. She *would* surely die, for she became mortal. Because Adam was in authority over her, choosing to partake of the fruit she gave him, he was held responsible for her sin whilst taking the punishment for his own. It is for this reason that the New Testament states that **For as in Adam all die, even so in Christ shall all be made alive** (1 Corinthians 15:22).

Adam was not deceived. Eve was. He voluntarily took of the fruit she offered, so as to share her fate. His love for her motivated him to become sin with her. Jesus is the last Adam. Like Adam, He was not deceived. Like Adam, His love for us motivated Him to become sin for us. They both sacrificed themselves for someone they loved. Jesus sacrificed Himself for you.

The serpent appealed to Eve's sense of avarice. She wanted to know more, to be productive, and to be highly esteemed. All she had to do was come out from under her husband's authority and seize the forbidden fruit. And seize it she did; **having taken of its fruit she ate** (Genesis 3:6b LXX). The serpent had effectively thwarted the chain of command. He targeted and disabled the woman who had left her spiritual protector at home. Please don't leave home without yours.

3) God's Safeguards for Women.

God commands us to adhere to the chain of command by submitting to our husbands in order to promote the following: a) power, b) peace, c) equality, d) trust, and e) reverence. The accompanying safeguards prevent f) adultery, g) jealousy and vain glory, h) dishonesty, i) blasphemy, and j) compromise.

This section will address these as they apply to the body of Christ, which is not only the individual, but the church of God.

a) The promotion of power

We know that **there is no power but of God: the powers that be are ordained of God** (Romans 13:1b). God has established the law, He has fulfilled the law, and His Word is law. Our job is to obey: **Let every soul**

be subject unto the higher powers (Romans 13:1a). If we search the Bible for the way power functions under God, we will understand that obedience offers much more power than disobedience. Here's how it works.

Paul, to the Corinthians, writes: **Every man praying or prophesying, having his head covered, dishonoureth his head: But every woman that prayeth or prophesieth with her head uncovered dishonoureth her head** (1 Corinthians 11:4-5). The head symbolizes authority: **the head of every man is Christ; and the head of the woman is the man; and the head of Christ is God** (1 Corinthians 11:3). To symbolize subordination to Christ, the man is to uncover his head. To symbolize subordination to her husband, the wife is to cover her head. As long as her head is "covered", she may pray or prophesy, and it will be both effective and pleasing to God. In other words, her prayers and prophesies will have potency; they will be heard and acted upon.

Paul goes on to teach that the woman is the glory of the man (1 Corinthians 11:7) and was created for the man (1 Corinthians 11:9). He then writes, **For this cause ought the woman to have power on her head because of the angels** (1 Corinthians 11:10). If a wife fulfills her role to glorify her husband by submitting herself to him, she has "power on her head". There is obviously a supernatural significance to the wife's observance of the command structure that involves the angels. This is fascinating, but not something that I am able to fully explain. What is clear from the text is that if a wife does not fulfill her role to glorify her husband and submit to him, she loses power.

The Bible explains that **Rightful rule gives power to words** (Proverbs 17:14a LXX). The woman who usurps her husband's authority, just like the woman who seizes authority in the church, does not have the "rightful rule". Her words (prophecies, prayers) are therefore powerless before God. **And if a man also strive for masteries, yet is he not crowned, except he strive lawfully** (2 Timothy 2:5). Her wrongfully seized authority is not recognized by the God she claims to serve. Consequently, God considers her prayers loathsome and defiled: **He that turns away his ear from hearing the law, even he has made his prayer abominable** (Proverbs 28:9 LXX).

Lawlessness and rebellion ruin the soul. Only an obedient, submissive woman has the power that accompanies naming the name of Christ as her Lord and Saviour.

b) The promotion of peace

Paul goes on further to say that **Nevertheless neither is the man without the woman, neither the woman without the man, in the Lord** (1 Corinthians 11:11). We are all one body in Christ. Maintaining the chain of command is essential to the peaceful functionality of the body. **For God is not the author of confusion, but of peace, as in all churches of the saints** (1 Corinthians 14:33). Peace is only possible through order.

This is illustrated in Paul's teachings about the body of Christ. He writes, **Now there are diversities of gifts, but the same Spirit. And there are differences in administrations, but the same Lord. And there are diversities of operations, but it is the same God which worketh all in all** (1 Corinthians 12:4-6). Although we are all members of the same body, we all have our realm of influence, which is a place, position, appointment, or rank within the body of Christ. It is a simple fact that we cannot all be the most **comely parts** (1 Corinthians 12:24).

Peace is maintained in both the church and the home when we are **of the same mind one toward another. Mind not high things, but condescend to men of low estate. Be not wise in your own conceits** (Romans 12:16). A usurper wants to be a leader, in condescension of the lower ranks. She applies superior status to leadership as though it is somehow more important or more valuable than the position of follower. This is the kind of worldly thinking that Jesus spoke against in Matthew 20:20-28 when the disciples were vying for the highest status in His kingdom, which they thought would be on earth. They associated greatness with authority and position instead of associating it with servitude. Jesus told them:

> **Ye know that the princes of the Gentiles exercise dominion over them, and they that are great exercise authority upon them. But it shall not be so among you: but whosoever will be great among you, let him be your minister; And whosoever will be chief among you, let him be your servant: Even as the Son of man came not to be ministered unto, but to minister, and to give his life a ransom for many** (Matthew 20:25-28).

The Jews were under Roman rule. Embittered by the harsh treatment that they received at the hands of "greater men", they wanted the tables to be turned so that they could have their chance to exercise dominion and authority over others. As revolutionaries, they thought Jesus' coming would provide that chance, proving that neither they nor their mother[19] understood the implications of their request. Jesus said, **Are ye able to drink of the cup that I shall drink of, and to be baptized with the baptism that I am baptized with? They say unto him, We are able** (Matthew 20:22). They thought themselves able to be leaders of men; in actuality, by being followers of Christ, they would suffer and die as slaves for the sake of the gospel. It is in this capacity as servants that the greatest rewards are received.

The usurping woman has been allured by the worldly rewards of high status and financial prosperity. She has been deceived. **Beware lest any man spoil you through philosophy and vain deceit, after the tradition of men, after the rudiments of the world, and not after Christ** (Colossians 2:8). Her reward, were she to submit herself willingly to Christ, would be far greater in heaven than anything she could ever experience here on earth. If she were truly great in the sight of the Lord, she would obey His Word and make herself a minister to others as **followers of that which is good** (1 Peter 3:13b).

Paul points out the absurdity of vying for the chief rank: **If the whole body were an eye, where were the hearing? If the whole were hearing, where were the smelling? But now hath God set the members every one of them in the body, as it hath pleased him** (1 Corinthians 12:17-18). Leaders and followers are co-dependent. One cannot exist without the other. We function as a team, according to our various gifts, and according to the will of God. A team needs a captain, an army needs a general, and a body needs a head. **For the husband is the head of the wife, even as**

---

[19] Matthew 20:20, "Then came the mother of Zebedee's children with her sons, worshipping him, and desiring a certain thing of him." That certain thing was this: "Grant that these my two sons may sit, the one on thy right hand, and the other on the left, in thy kingdom" (vs. 21). Remember that at the time, the disciples thought that Jesus would save the Jews from Roman tyranny to become King of the Jews. They were not yet aware that Christ's kingdom is the kingdom of heaven.

Christ is the head of the church (Ephesians 5:23a). Each part is both necessary and valuable. None is irrelevant or expendable.

The usurper is not content with her position in the body and would thwart the peaceful co-existence of the church and home in order to fulfill her ambitious agenda. Paul wrote, **I have learned, in whatsoever state I am, therewith to be content** (Philippians 4:11).

c) The promotion of equality

The God who said, **Husbands, love your wives, even as Christ also loved the church, and gave himself for it** (Ephesians 5:25) is the same God who defends women as His own daughters, having died for them just as much as He died for men. **So ought men to love their wives as their own bodies. He that loveth his wife loveth himself. For no man ever hateth his own flesh; but nourisheth it and cherisheth it, even as the Lord the church: For we are members of his body, of his flesh, and of his bones** (Ephesians 5:28-30). This is a profound blessing; one which could only come from an all-loving and all-powerful Father-God.

Husbands and wives are **heirs together of the grace of life** (1 Peter 3:7b). They are of equal value in the sight of the Lord. **There is neither male nor female: for ye are all one in Christ Jesus** (Galatians 3:28).

d) The promotion of trust

In the old time, the holy women also, who trusted in God adorned themselves, being in subjection to their own husbands (1 Peter 3:51). These women were not subject because they had poor social status.[20] It is

---

[20] If high social status was relative to a woman's opportunity to wield power and influence, Jezebel, the Queen, Deborah, the Judge, and Ana, the Prophetess would not exist as examples of extremely powerful women who lived in Bible times. Acts 17 refers to "chief women" (vs. 4) and "honourable women" (vs. 12) who lived among the Greeks, and these examples are only a few of many, from various cultures. Obviously, the general opinion that women's social status was low in Bible times is presumptuous, flawed, and misleading. For as long as women have attained wisdom and understanding, inspired confidence and

not because they were ignorant, unlearned, or incapable. It is certainly not because their opinions were invalid. It is because these early "church" women trusted in God. They feared Him and loved Him enough to obey His commandments. They did not question His method or the validity of the rules. They trusted in His infinite wisdom, knowing that He was in control. As a result, they were called *holy*.

Sara exemplified this holiness by calling her husband Abraham, "lord", a sign of her submission to him as well as her trust in him. We are her daughters—that is, followers of her godly example—**as long as ye do well, and are not afraid with any amazement** (1 Peter 3:6b). Trust is the key.

To fear the Lord is to recognize His power. To be amazed is to be in awe of something without being able to fully comprehend it. Sara practised a godly fear of her husband because she understood what it meant to fear the Lord. She was afraid—with understanding. As her daughters, we are to fear our husbands with the same fear of the Lord that that understanding implies. It implies an implicit and wholesome trust in God.

Isaiah wrote, **Behold, my God is my Saviour; I will trust in him, and not be afraid: for the Lord is my glory and my praise, and is become my salvation** (Isaiah 12:2 LXX). Many of us are afraid to trust our husbands. However, the Lord delivers us from such fear because of our understanding. King David said **The Lord is my light and my Saviour; whom shall I fear? the Lord is the defender of my life; of whom shall I be afraid?** (Psalm 27:1 LXX). When we trust God, we have absolutely nothing to fear from man. **Though an army should set itself in array against me, my heart shall not be afraid** (Psalm 27:3a LXX).

Your trust in God will never confound (amaze or confuse) you (Psalm 25:2 LXX). It will never be in vain. Paul wrote to Timothy, **For therefore we both labour and suffer reproach, because we trust in the living God, who is the Saviour of all men, especially of those that believe** (1 Timothy 4:10). While those around you may wonder why you treat your

---

peace, they have wielded influence. The nature of women has not changed; the only thing that has changed is the conspicuous positions of authority that women hold today. Even Abigail, whose husband was a foolish oaf, had the authority to rectify his insult to David. No matter how large or small your "realm" is, as a wife, you are still its queen.

undeserving husband so well, even mocking or disdaining you for it, your Father in heaven will crown you with glory because you have trusted in Him.

By trusting in God, in His Word, and in His promises, we have no reason to be amazed or uncertain about following His holy and ordained power structure. Our purpose in obeying the commands to be silent and in subjection is to reflect our fear of God, which is not the end of wisdom, but the beginning. This understanding lends itself to godly confidence and integrity, and an unwavering trust in God.

e) The promotion of reverence

And the wife, see that she reverence her husband (Ephesians 5:33b). In 1st Timothy 2, we are given the perfect model of how to show reverence to our husbands. Paul begins the passage with an exhortation to us to pray for those who are in authority over us. He writes

> **I exhort therefore, that, first of all, supplications, prayers, intercessions, and giving of thanks, be made for all men; For kings and all that are in authority; that we may lead a quiet and peaceable life in all godliness and honesty. For this is good and acceptable in the sight of God our Saviour** (1 Timothy 2:1-3).

Not only are we to adhere to the rank structure as it has been ordained by God, but we are also to pray for *all* in authority over us, which includes our husbands. We are to pray for them with thankfulness. By so doing, we are assured of a quiet and peaceable life that is both godly and honest. By practising gratitude in our hearts as we pray daily for our husbands, we form the habit of thinking kindly on them. We prove by our grateful prayers to God for our husbands that we accept subordination as a privilege and a blessing. This is a form of reverence which not only shows that our heads are "covered", but also that God is pleased by it, calling it "good and acceptable".

1 Timothy 2 continues with further instruction about how we are to defer to our husband's authority, in corroboration with 1 Corinthians 14.

Women **are to learn in silence with all subjection** (1 Timothy 2:11). If women want to **learn any thing, let them ask their husbands at home** (1 Corinthians 14:35a). This is the doctrinal chain of command. In keeping it, women give their husbands reverence by refraining from usurping authority over them (1Timothy 2:10).

What? came the word of God out from you? or came it unto you only? (1 Corinthians 14:36). Paul reminds the Gentiles that they were not the "chosen people"—the primary recipients of God's Word. For the Gentiles who in Paul's day did not have the Hebrew tradition, their training in spiritual matters came from the apostles. In the same way, a wife's training is to come from her husband. As Adam received God's instructions and taught them to Eve, so a husband is to study the Word and know it well enough to teach it to his own wife. A wife reverences her husband when she looks to him as her teacher, leader, and spiritual head. A wife dishonours her husband when she elevates her own spirituality over his.[21]

For a man indeed ought not to cover his head, forasmuch as he is the image and glory of God: but the woman is the glory of the man . . . . Neither was the man created for the woman; but the woman for the man (1 Corinthians 11:7, 9). A woman does not give her husband glory by disrupting Bible studies with many questions which reveal that he failed to teach her at home. Nor does she give her husband glory if she "proves" herself spiritually superior in public by answering other people's questions without deferring to him first. No matter how gifted she is in spiritual understanding, her job is not to take the glory for herself. She is to give it to her husband. She accomplishes this by keeping silent in the church, in obedience to God's Word.

This is the essence of voluntary—even cheerful—submission. Her silence is proof of her refusal to usurp her husband's authority. An open discussion at home between husband and wife is acceptable, because as long as it is respectful, it facilitates learning. Such a discussion at church is not acceptable because **it is a shame for women to speak in the church** (1 Corinthians 14:35b).

---

[21] Remember that a woman's expression of spirituality differs from a man's. While she is generally more emotional and verbal in her expression, he is not. This difference in no way indicates that he is less spiritual.

There are cases in which a woman is not only able to teach, but is commanded to do so. As long as her intention is not to usurp authority but to give her husband and God glory, women such as Deborah[22] and Priscilla [23] qualify as "Titus 2" teachers whom Paul describes in the following verses:

> **The aged women likewise, that they be in behaviour as becometh holiness, not false accusers, not given to much wine, teachers of good things; That they may teach the young women to be sober, to love their husbands, to love their children, To be discreet, chaste, keepers at home, good, obedient to their own husbands, that the word of God be not blasphemed** (Titus 2:3-5).

Women who live these verses are qualified by their godly obedience and wisdom to teach other women—not men. No woman can ever be "qualified" to disobey God by becoming a preacher.[24] She can speak of the Lord to all those who look for redemption (Luke 2:38), but she cannot take on the formal duties of a church leader. A Titus 2 woman teaches other women how to guide their home in a way that brings them godly joy and blessing. This is the way of God's will.

i) Deborah

Matthew 20:25 tells us about the way the Gentiles practised authority and dominion in the time of Jesus—a model that is practised by our culture today. They sought high status through conspicuous achievement, then "lorded" it over others. This kind of leadership was not practised traditionally by the Jews. In Deborah's time, before there were kings in Israel, her position as judge came in recognition of her wisdom. She did

---

22 See full story in Judges 4 and 5.
23 Priscilla and Aquila, a married couple, assisted as "fellow workers" in Paul's ministry to the church. See Acts 18 and 1 Corinthians 16:19.
24 By "preacher", I mean the official spiritual leader of a church who teaches both men and/or women Bible doctrine and/or performs the sacraments of marriage, baptism, or communion.

not seek the position for purposes of gain or glory. She did not curry favour or utter "campaign promises" in order to secure her status. She was awarded the "office" because of her Titus 2 qualifications. People came to her because she was wise and knew the will of God.

In 1 Corinthians 6, Paul chastises the church for bringing disputes before unbelieving judges instead of seeking judgment from wise men of the church (1 Corinthians 6:1). He said, **If then ye have judgments pertaining to things of this life, set them to judge who are least esteemed in the church. I speak to your shame. Is it so, that there is not a wise man among you?** (1 Corinthians 6:4-5a). Paul calls it shameful because even the least spiritually wise member of the church is wiser than the worldly unbeliever, and therefore able to judge "things of this life". The point of interest in this passage is that judges were set over worldly matters, not church matters. The priests led the church. Similarly, Deborah heard civil matters and resolved disputes. She sat under a tree and people came to her for judgment (Judges 4:4-5 LXX). This is the function of a "Judge". She did not teach men doctrine.

Deborah was a prophetess. In the Old Testament, before the Bible was collated, a prophet or prophetess proclaimed God's will to people in a revelatory manner. They were not leaders of the people. On the contrary, many were persecuted and killed for speaking the truth in warning. Deborah had no intention of leading the Israelites. Barak was the appointed head of the Israelite army and Deborah knew that it was his job to lead, a fact that she was quick to remind him of: **Has not the Lord God of Israel commanded *thee*?** (Judges 4:6b LXX, emphasis mine). It was clear from her actions that Deborah did not seek glory.[25] She was not a usurper. She was a godly woman who wisely feared the Lord.

In the end, Barak brought Deborah with him to the battlefield contrary to the command of God. As a result, the glory of the Israelite victory over Sisera was given to a woman (Judges 4:9 LXX). The purpose of this was not to relieve Barak of his responsibilities but to punish him for his cowardice. Whenever a woman takes the glory that God intended for a man, that man is put to shame.

---

[25]   In Judges 5, she and Barak sing glory to God for the victory.

ii) Priscilla

Priscilla was the godly wife of a godly Jewish man named Aquila. They helped Paul labour in the Word together (Romans 16:3). They expounded scriptures together (Acts 18:26), travelled as missionaries together (Acts 18:18), and hosted a house church together (1 Corinthians 16:19). When an eloquent and persuasive speaker named Apollos delivered a powerful message to the Jews at synagogue, Aquila and Priscilla were listening (Acts 18:26). Realizing that he had been baptized by John, but did not yet know Christ crucified, *they* approached him after church, took him into their home, and **expounded unto him the way of God more perfectly** (Acts 18:26b).

This is a beautiful example of how a Titus 2 woman can support her husband in wisdom and understanding without usurping his authority. Because Priscilla did not have the heart of a usurper, the chain of command remained unbroken and God's will for women was upheld and sustained in her marriage. Their ministry was blessed because **It is not good that the man should be alone** (Genesis 2:18a LXX). When he marries a godly woman, he has been given **a help suitable to him** (Genesis 2:18b LXX). God uses women to accomplish good and wonderful things *if* she practises a modest, sober, and godly reverence for her husband.

If King Solomon could not find a single wise woman among 1,000 (Ecclesiastes 7:27-28 LXX), how rare do you think Titus 2 women like Deborah and Priscilla are in today's church? If your church allows women to speak, would a true Titus 2 woman seize that opportunity? With gentle persuasion, would she speak? How about with urgent appeal? Perhaps if the elders of the church insisted the way Barak did with Deborah would she speak. She would get up to say something similar to what Deborah said: "Didn't God command *men* to lead this church?" Maybe she would say what Paul said: "I speak to your shame". A true Titus 2 woman knows that it is a shame for women to speak in the church. **Therefore to him that knoweth to do good, and doeth it not, to him it is sin** (James 4:17).

Many women in today's church masquerade as Titus 2 mentors. Pay attention to the way a self-professed Titus 2 woman treats her husband. If she rules the roost, taking the glory that is meant for her husband for herself, she is not a Titus 2 woman, and there is nothing of value for you to learn from her.

A woman who reverences her husband is wise because the desire of her heart is to obey the Word of God. It is obedience to God's Word that makes us wise, but too few of us obey. Obedience is essential: she that "hearkens" to wisdom **shall dwell in confidence, and shall rest securely from all evil** (Proverbs 1:33 LXX). A wise woman understands that there is only one unfailing source of wisdom, which is God's redemptive truth as told from Genesis to Revelation. She fears God too much to question the rules. She accepts them because they come from a Holy God who knows infinitely more than she does. She is **under obedience, as also saith the law . . .**

If any man think himself to be a prophet, or spiritual, let him acknowledge that the things that I write unto you are the commandments of the Lord. But if any man be ignorant, let him be ignorant (1 Corinthians 34b, 37-38). In other words, a Christian who is inspired by the Holy Spirit or who is gifted in prophecy, when reading these verses, will acknowledge that they come directly from God. A disobedient and lawless individual, on the other hand, who lacks spiritual depth and understanding, will remain ignorant in her ways, wasting time fighting over words and interpretations that bring further ungodliness instead of receiving the blessings that result from embracing and obeying the plain truth of God's infallible Word.

When you choose to reverence your husband as unto Christ, you are placing your trust and hope wholly in God. When an occasion arises for you to speak, keep silent. Trust that God has given you this command not to strip you of your own power, but to adorn you with His.

f) The prevention of adultery

Remember that submission and self-denial for the sake of Christ and His church bring edification and joy. By obeying His Word, we subvert danger and receive blessings.

Not every woman who disobeys God's Word and gives reverence to another man will commit adultery just like not all children who disobey their parents and play on the road will be hit by a car. I believe that when God told us to learn from our husbands at home, He did so to safeguard our marriage as well as to safeguard that of others. In turn, the sanctity, unity, and fellowship of the church body are preserved.

Have you ever looked upon a strong male spiritual leader or teacher with respect, deference, or affection? A woman can be drawn to strong, "respectable" preachers, speakers, or Bible teachers who appear to be more "spiritual" than their own husbands. She might ask him Bible or marriage-related questions after church or through other media. By so doing, she is giving the respect that belongs to her husband to another man.

This is not to say that her intentions are wholly misguided. Certainly not do all women who seek Biblical teaching from godly men purpose in their hearts to commit adultery. However, it has happened far too often that even the best of intentions lead to disaster.

The Bible says that even to look upon another person lustfully is to commit adultery in your heart (Matthew 5:28). Lust is not limited to sexual desire; the lust of the flesh refers to all things that are consumed by the Self and sought from the world. The desire to attain Biblical knowledge from a man other than your husband is dangerous. What too few women realize is that asking a man for advice is a form of reverence. When a married woman does this to someone other than her husband, she is deferring to another man's authority, which is an adulterous act.

For example, when King Ahaziah fell through a lattice in his upper room and got sick, he sought advice regarding the outcome of his condition. Instead of showing loyalty and respect to God's authority by seeking His advice, he chose to seek advice from the false god, Baalzebub (2 Kings 1:2 LXX). What was God's response to that "adulterous" act?

> **And an angel of the Lord called [Elijah], saying, Arise, and go to meet the messengers of [King Ahaziah], and thou shalt say to them, Is it because there is no God in Israel, that ye go to enquire of [Baalzebub]? but it shall not be so. For thus saith the Lord, The bed on which thou art gone up, thou shalt not come down from it, for thou shalt surely die. And [Elijah] went, and said so to them . . . . So [King Ahaziah] died according to the word of the Lord which [Elijah] had spoken** (2 Kings 1:3-4, 17 LXX).

When you have a father or husband as your spiritual head to seek advice from, it is inappropriate for you to seek advice from another man. Remember, God's Word tells us to obey our *own* husbands,[26] not somebody else's! We are not to give reverence through obedience to another man.

A married man who receives reverence from another woman is presented with a stumbling-block: by receiving a form of glory from another woman, he becomes emotionally disposed to her, and naturally affectionate towards her. If he is unlucky enough to have an irreverent wife, he will be weak, and therefore susceptible to the temptation presented by a more reverent woman. For this reason, unsupervised counselling between a male pastor and a female parishioner is intolerable.

Reverencing and obeying your *own* husband is an act of endearment, and it blesses your husband, glorifies God, and makes your home happy. These rewards are gifts that the Lord gives to those who love and obey Him, and who trust in Him by submitting to their *own* husbands.

g) The prevention of jealousy and vain glory

Jealousy and strife ensue in the churches that sacrifice the Word of God for the ego of women. It has happened far too often. Here is an example of how it works.

A usurper feels justified by her good works. She enjoys the glory that accompanies public approval. When she is asked to speak or to present on some of her work, she takes the opportunity to prove the value of her labours. She is too smitten by pride to question her motives.

After her first time speaking, she receives attention and acclamation. Women seek her out after the service to congratulate and encourage her efforts. Her pride has tasted the forbidden fruit, and she develops an appetite for it.

Other women in the congregation witness her tasty bite of the forbidden fruit and want some of the same. They, too, have performed good works, and they, too, feel that they should be given an opportunity to speak about it. While the Holy Spirit may prick their consciences, the fact that another woman spoke and received praise for it emboldens them to speak, too.

---

[26] Ephesians 5:22, 4, Colossians 3:18, Titus 2:5, 1 Peter 3:1, 5

They begin to plot ways to stand up or at the front to speak. They discuss other women's speaking abilities and start throwing around words like, "gifted speaker", "teacher", or "Titus 2 woman". A pecking order is established, with the most "spiritual" woman on top. She becomes the most popular woman in the church and boasts in her heart that she must therefore be a "Titus 2" woman.

> **For all their works they do for to be seen of men: they make broad their phylacteries,**[27] **and enlarge the borders of their garments, And love the uppermost rooms at feasts, and the chief seats in the synagogues, And greetings in the markets, and to be called of men, Rabbi, Rabbi. But be not ye called Rabbi: for one is your Master, even Christ; and all ye are brethren** (Matthew 23:5-8).

A rebellious and competitive spirit infects the women in the church. Self-will and vanity are hidden beneath a "religious" guise wherein a community of usurpers begin to set the church standards. Like the Pharisees, **This people draweth nigh unto me with their mouth, and honoureth me with their lips; but their heart is far from me. But in vain do they worship me, teaching for doctrines the commandments of men** (Matthew 15:8-9). What these women may not realize is that they have become usurpers puffed up on pride and vanity. Their motivation is based on a vain desire for glory. They are not following the way of Christ; they are following the way of the world. They blindly cause others to do the same.

> **Who is a wise man and endued**[28] **with knowledge among you? Let him shew out of a good conversation his works with meekness of wisdom. But if ye have bitter envying**

---

[27] Essentially, this means that they pride themselves on knowing each and every detail of the law. Their garments were embroidered with laws. The broader the garment, the more laws could be fit on it and seen by the public as examples of their outstanding piety. Not every woman who takes the time and effort to memorize Bible verses does so to please God. The usurper does so out of the vain desire to impress others and to prove herself more "spiritual" than they.

[28] "Endued" means infused, taken on.

and strife in your hearts, glory not, and lie not against the truth. This wisdom descendeth not from above, but is earthly, sensual, devilish. For where envying and strife is, there is confusion and every evil work (James 3:13-15).

It is not wrong for a godly woman to cultivate the desire to serve God and to act on that desire within her God-given sphere of influence. However, the usurper is not a godly woman; she is a "religious" woman. She seeks glory in the same way that the Pharisees did. James says, **If any man among you seem to be religious, and bridleth not his tongue, but deceiveth his own heart, this man's religion is vain** (James 1:26).

If a church permits women in leadership, how many of the women who agree to take part are godly and how many are "religious"? How is a church to exercise faithful quality control in such a situation? There is but one way: by obeying God's Word and insisting with uncompromising integrity that women keep silent in the church.

When women in church put themselves forward to earn worldly rewards by seizing positions of leadership, the church will plummet into spiritual numbness. **Can the blind lead the blind? shall they not both fall into the ditch?** (Luke 6:39). The men start believing that faith is for women and the women are so distracted by trying to out-do one another that they forget whom they serve. Such a church is out of order. It is fruitless and it is spiritually dead or dying because it is operating outside the will of God. The natural consequence of the usurper's sin is the defilement of the church.

h) The prevention of dishonesty

The usurper often seizes authority based on spiritually unverifiable "intuition", without realizing that what she is really calling on are the unbiblical role reversals that have been programmed into her by feminist media. By falling prey to the devil's deceptive lies, she has become one of **those that oppose themselves** (2 Timothy 2:25); one who is in the **snare of the devil, who are taken captive by him at his will** (2 Timothy 2:26b). Being taken captive by the devil, at his will and not your own, is the Biblical definition of brainwashing.

The usurper, having been deceived into believing herself entitled to take a position of higher authority in the church or home, repeats the same lies that the devil has told her. As we learned in the previous chapter, God hates liars. When a liar and usurper reign, the church and home are rendered unproductive and unfruitful because the chain of command has been broken. **Blessed are the blameless in the way, who walk in the law of the Lord** (Psalm 119:1 LXX).

When a woman chooses to be in obedience to the Word of God, she is convicted by the verses that prohibit usurpation. As such, she can identify that the imaginations of her heart are unreliable (Jeremiah 3:17 LXX), and can bring them under submission to Christ (1 Corinthians 10:5). This is honest.

i) The prevention of blasphemy

Believing servants, slaves, and all those who are under authority, including women, are told to **count their own masters worthy of all honour, that the name of God and his doctrine be not blasphemed** (1 Timothy 6:1). Similarly, in Titus 2, women are told to be **obedient to their own husbands, that the word of God be not blasphemed** (Titus 2:5b). We have already learned that the usurping of authority renders our words and prayers loathsome, but now we learn that such lawless ambition brings evil upon God's Name and God's Word.

Women who disobey God by becoming preachers believe and/or claim that they are answering God's "call" to preach. This could not be further from the truth. The Holy Spirit does not call us to disobedience; the spirit of rebellion does. If a female preacher says that she was called by God, not only is she a liar, but she is also committing blasphemy by calling that which is evil, good.

God addresses such people in Jeremiah 23:

> **Therefore, behold, I am against the prophets that prophesy false dreams, and have not told them truly, and have caused my people to err by their lies, and by their errors; yet I sent them not, and commanded them not; therefore, they shall not profit this people at all. And if this people, or the priest,**

> **or the prophet, should ask, What is the burden of the Lord? then thou shalt say to them, Ye are the burden, and I will dash you down, saith the Lord** (Jeremiah 23:32-33 LXX).

What a valuable witness you are to the perfect will of Christ and the joy of subservience when you live in obedient submission to God and to your husband.

j) The prevention of compromise

Because many of those around the usurper have been similarly brainwashed by a secular media that promotes a feminist agenda, even the men appointed to lead the church by upholding the Word concede to her self-appointed, media-induced, moral "high ground". These men are deceived, thinking that their philanthropic efforts toward women are moral and helpful. On the contrary, such negligence enables and abets the usurper's disobedience.

While they fail to safeguard the church, these men live with blinders on as those who seek worldly popularity over godly approbation: **For do I now persuade men, or God? or do I seek to please men? for if I yet pleased men, I should not be the servant of Christ** (Galatians 1:10). In their support of a feminist agenda, they concede to **seducing spirits, and doctrines of devils** (1 Timothy 4:1b).

The servant of Christ follows Him, His Word, and His way. Those who promote the interests of the female usurpers along with the usurpers themselves have built their houses upon the sand. Instead of building firmly upon the Word, they have fallen on the sand of compromise. Social niceties and sycophantic favours shroud the disharmony and disorder that reign in the church that has fallen away from the will of God.

Women are to have a **meek and quiet spirit** (1 Peter 3:4). They are to have **shamefacedness and sobriety** (1 Timothy 2:9). The boldness, loudness, and competitiveness of the usurper are unattractive, unfeminine, and unfulfilling. The further a woman departs from the Word and will of God in this regard, the more fleeting will true happiness, beauty, and joy become. To excuse, compromise, or render Biblical guidelines flexible or partial is to starve your soul of the very thing it requires for sustenance.

The point is not only to obey, but to obey happily: **serve the Lord with gladness and a good heart** (Deuteronomy 28:47b LXX). Just as we offer our tithes, recognizing how fleeting worldly wealth is, so we give of our*selves* in recognition of the fact that at any time our life could be over, and with it, our chance to serve. **Every man according as he purposeth in his heart, so let him give; not grudgingly, or of necessity: for God loveth a cheerful giver** (2 Corinthians 9:6-7). Grudging, resentful submission is not submission at all. It is defiant compliance offered along with a punishing dose of emotional fallout. Obedience rendered in this ungodly form is a curse, and it makes the home a sullen and miserable place to be.

And let the peace of God rule in your hearts, to the which also ye are called in one body; and be ye thankful (Colossians 3:15). Peace and productivity can only reign when each member of the body of Christ functions within her established parameters. God's parameters for women are glorious if they are kept. The godliest women are not those who stand in front of the largest crowd, broadcasting live before the whole world. **For what shall it profit a man, if he shall gain the whole world, and lose his own soul?** (Mark 8:36). The godliest women are those who value what Christ values—**the ornament of a meek and quiet spirit** (1 Peter 3:4b).

James says, **Pure religion and undefiled before God and the Father is this, To visit the fatherless and widows in their affliction, and to keep himself unspotted from the world** (James 1:27). Serve the Lord peaceably and gladly, with humility and submission. Only then will your soul be prospered, your marriage blessed, and your spirit fruitful.

Modern Snapshot
DEBBIE

It all began after Debbie had her first child. Debbie had always tried to be obedient and respectful to her husband, but after her son was born, she felt that she had a higher calling. She felt that she had insight into the needs of her infant that her husband did not, and she began to lord it over him.

Her husband's bad habits, which bothered her only mildly before, suddenly loomed over her with overwhelming foreboding. She translated his faults into future calamities that would surely befall his son if they were not stopped. Puffing herself up on self-righteous indignation, she took it upon herself to change his ways.

She started by keeping a watchful eye on every move he made with their son. She peered over his shoulder as he bathed him, making curt suggestions and not-so-friendly criticisms. She clucked with impatience when he struggled to fasten the baby's diaper. She seethed in anger when he failed to pick up the crying infant in the middle of the night when it was his watch.

Despite her suggestions and genuine attempts to show her husband the "best" way to do things, he was not improving. On the contrary, Debbie soon discovered that her husband was not only resistant to her suggestions, but was also openly avoiding her. He was distracted and disinterested. Instead of relying on her to make the best decisions for their son, her husband started relying on his mother. He brought her into the home regularly, forcing Debbie to take third place.

Sensing her increasing loss of control, Debbie began using different ploys to compel her husband's cooperation. She proved herself efficient and capable in many areas, hoping to impress upon him her abilities. However, along with her change in attitude came a diminished respect for her husband.

Soon, when speaking to friends and family, she found herself vilifying him by exaggerating his deficiencies. She became haughty and disagreeable with him in public, seeking social pressure to shame him into compliance.

Her pride refused to break, but every night she cried herself to sleep. She knew that she was losing the battle, and that neither God nor her husband were on her side.

One day, Debbie, her husband, and their nine-month old son went out for dinner together. They had leg of lamb. Even though the baby was given breast-milk only, Debbie's husband decided to give him a lamb bone to chew on. When Debbie saw her son smearing bits of meat and fat all over his little face, she reacted. She did everything she could to persuade her husband to remove the offensive object. Unperturbed, he left the bone where it was. He had had enough of her attempts to control him. Debbie shed a torrent of tears to reveal to him the depth of her dismay. Her wise husband ignored her.

On the way home from that dinner, it occurred to a teary-eyed, prayerful Debbie that she had been trying to usurp her husband's authority. She revisited the actions and inactions of the past several months in her mind, identifying them for what they were. This time, she shed the sincere tears of repentance. Thankfully, her husband quickly forgave her, and they moved on. Because he had refused to be subordinated, resisting her attempts to take over his authority, he was able to facilitate her change of heart. Debbie learned her lesson, thanked the Lord, and went on to experience a blessed marriage.

> **I have set before you life and death,**
> **the blessing and the curse:**
> **choose thou life, that thou and thy seed may live;**
> **to love the Lord thy God, to hearken to his voice, and**
> **cleave to him;**
> **for this is thy life, and the length of thy days**
> (Deuteronomy 30:19b-20a LXX).

Summary

Instead of cleaving to that which is good, and promised by God, a usurping woman caters to the virtues that are prescribed by a dead and dying world of lost sinners. Lacking wisdom, deceived by the devil's lies, she does not value the things that are above. **If ye then be risen with Christ, seek those things which are above, where Christ sitteth on the right hand of God** (Colossians 3:1).

A usurping woman values the conspicuous symbols of worldly clout and earthly wisdom that are below. If in this capacity, she claims to be answering God's call to preach or lead, she is a liar and a blasphemer. She will be nothing more than a "blind leader of the blind". **And if the blind lead the blind, both shall fall into the ditch** (Matthew 15:14b).

Usurping women neither understand nor respect the mind of Christ. They have a Bible available to them which they might read from time to time, but they do not take to heart the words that lie therein nor the Source from whom those words have come. **And the fruit of righteousness is sown in peace of them that make peace** (James 3:18).

Who Shall Deliver Me?

- **Therefore thus saith the Holy One of Israel, Because ye have refused to obey these words, and have trusted in falsehood; and because thou hast murmured, and been confident in this respect: therefore shall this sin be to you as a wall suddenly fallen when a strong city has been taken, of which the fall is very near at hand** (Isaiah 30:12 LXX).
- **The Lord is not slack concerning his promise, as some men count slackness; but is longsuffering to us-ward, not willing that any should perish, but that all should come to repentance** (2 Peter 3:9).
- **Nevertheless the foundation of God standeth sure, having this seal, The Lord knoweth them that are his. And, Let every one that nameth the name of Christ depart from iniquity** (2 Timothy 2:19).
- **In God will we make our boast all the day, and to thy name will we give thanks forever** (Psalm 44:8 LXX).

How Can I Be Humble?

- Be sober (Romans 12:3).
- Be vigilant (1 Peter 5:8).
- Be not deceived (2 Thessalonians 2:3).
- Rescind the authority that you have wrongfully seized from your husband (1 Peter 3:1).
- Cut out worldly influences from your life (Romans 13:14).
- Daily read and memorize the Word of God (Psalm 119:11 LXX).
- If you are asked to speak in church for any reason, say no, and be ready to explain your answer (1 Timothy 2:12).

Think on These Things

1. *Am I free to do anything as long as I want to serve God?*
   Gal. 5:13, 1 Peter 2:16

2. *How can I know what God's will is?*
   Luke 6:43, Gal. 5:22-23

3. *What is the order of authority in my family?*
   Eph. 5:23-24, 1 Cor. 11:3

4. *How can I change my feelings?*
   1 Peter 5:7, Phil. 2:2,5,13

5. *Why can't I trust my own feelings?*
   Phil. 3:3, 1 Cor. 13:12

6. *How does God want me to serve Him?*
   1 Tim. 2:15

7. *What is my true hope?*
   1 Peter 1:21, Ps. 119:114

8. *Why do I need God's armour?*
   Eph. 6:11

9. *How do I withstand accusations?*
   Eph. 6:16, Matt. 11:29

10. *Why should I submit and obey?*
    Heb. 13:17, James 3:14

CHAPTER SEVEN

THE SNARE IS BROKEN
PSALM 124:7 LXX

Our soul has been delivered as a sparrow from the snare of the fowlers: the snare is broken, and we are delivered (Psalm 124:7 LXX). I think you could use some deliverance by now! I have focused on the negative for a long time. It is time to change to the positive.

In this chapter, we will define the attributes of a **full soul** (Proverbs 27:7a LXX). A full soul is a prospered soul, which God gives us for our selfless service to Him. A full soul has her eyes set on Christ in singleness of heart and mind. She is set on perfection. She is blessed. **Come, hear, and I will tell, all ye that fear God, how great things he has done for my soul** (Psalm 66:16 LXX).

STUDY BREAK
Alas My Soul! (Micah 7:1 LXX)

The word "soul" appears in the KJ Bible 432 times. In the same way that the word "heart" was searched in Chapter Two, the "soul" search is accomplished and recorded here.

A soul is life. It can be quickened, delivered, restored, redeemed, ransomed, healed, kept, preserved, soothed, saved, and rescued. It can be prospered, filled, rested, or recompensed.

A soul can be destroyed, delivered to death, or consumed by fire. It can be pained, grieved, wearied, trampled, troubled, or embittered. It can be brought down to dust, bowed down, or passed into irons. It faints, fails, wants, desires, slumbers, weeps, pours out, or gets cut off. Troubles melt and vex it. A soul meditates unrighteous thoughts. It sins and brings destruction upon itself.

A soul knows, hungers, thirsts, longs, and pants for sustenance. It can be healed, comforted, satisfied, exalted, anchored, and lifted up. It can be cared for. It can be loved.

A soul can hear and obey the Lord. It can discern. It can receive counsel and be crafty. A soul can be wise. It can be spoken to. It can be humbled or haughty. It can be honoured or blessed. There is power and might in the soul.

A soul can be hunted, ensnared, persecuted, sought after, falsely accused, or plotted against. A soul can be unpitied. It can groan aloud. It can be removed from peace or brought out of affliction. A soul can be pierced, and is within reach of a sword.

Fleshly lusts war against the soul. Fruits can be departed from it; a record can be placed upon it. It can be deprived or defiled. A soul can hate itself.

The soul of the Lord takes pleasure in the righteous, but will be avenged on the unrighteous. Souls can wait for the Lord, hope in the Lord, boast in the Lord, rejoice in the Lord, praise the Lord, and magnify the Lord. Souls long for judgment. All souls belong to God.

Profile #7: The Full Soul
Blessed art thou Among Women (Luke 1:28)
MARY, THE MOTHER OF JESUS

The first thing I want to say about Mary, the mother of Jesus, is that she was an ordinary woman just like you or me. Although she was a godly woman highly favoured by God, she is not divine and she is not the **queen of heaven** (Jeremiah 44:18 LXX). What made her extraordinary, and the one Biblical woman whose positive example we should all follow, was her desire to do the will of God.

We meet Mary as a young virgin promised in marriage to a **just man** named Joseph, who was of the line of David (Matthew 1:19). **The angel Gabriel was sent from God** (Luke 1:26a) to greet Mary and give her the kind of news that no other woman has ever received. He said, **Hail, thou that art highly favoured, the Lord is with thee: blessed art thou among women** (Luke 1:28b).

Mary was **troubled at his saying, and cast in her mind what manner of salutation this should be** (Luke 1:29). Gabriel calmed her and told her that she was about to be the mother of Jesus, a child who **shall be great, and shall be called the Son of the Highest: and the Lord God shall give unto him the throne of his father David: And he shall reign over the house of Jacob for ever; and of his kingdom there shall be no end** (Luke 1:32-33).

Mary responded with, **How shall this be, seeing I know not a man?** (Luke 1:34b). After Gabriel explained, Mary replied, **Behold the handmaid of the Lord; be it unto me according to thy word** (Luke 1:38a).

Mary hasted to visit her cousin, Elisabeth, who was six months pregnant at the time (Luke 1:36). After their greetings were exchanged, Elisabeth said to Mary, **And blessed is she that believed: for there shall be a performance of those things which were told her from the Lord** (Luke 1:45).

The following verses give us an example to live by. They reveal Mary's heart:

> **And Mary said, My soul doth magnify the Lord, And my spirit hath rejoiced in God my Saviour. For he hath regarded the low estate of his handmaiden: for, behold, from henceforth all generations shall call me blessed. For he that is mighty hath done to me great things; and holy is his name. And his mercy is on them that fear him from generation to generation.**
>
> **He hath shewed strength with his arm; he hath scattered the proud in the imagination of their hearts. He hath put down the mighty from their seats, and exalted them of low degree. He hath filled the hungry with good things; and the rich he hath sent empty away. He hath holpen[1] his servant Israel, in remembrance of his mercy; As he spake**

---

[1] has helped

to our fathers, to Abraham, and to his seed forever (Luke 1:46-55, paragraph break mine).

How Can My Soul Be Filled?

A prospered soul never hungers. It is thoroughly satisfied and filled to overflowing. It never looks to itself to be filled, but to the Lord. Only God can fill your soul to overflowing. This chapter will show you how, contextualized by Mary's example.

There are seven positive actions that we can take towards the prospering of our souls. All are imperatives:

1. **Believe me** (John 14:11).
2. **Fear me** (Jeremiah 32:39 LXX).
3. **Hearken to me** (Leviticus 26:14 LXX).
4. **Learn of me** (Matthew 11:29).
5. **Love me** (John 14:23).
6. **Follow me** (John 10:27).
7. **Abide in me** (John 15:4).

In this chapter, we will briefly study each of these. In so doing, it is my hope and prayer for you that you will come to learn what it truly means to be a prosperous Christian. I can assure you that this prosperity is not the experience of having material wealth, personal power, clout, or popularity. Christian prosperity—true prosperity—is the experience of having a filled soul.

1. **Believe me** (John 14:11).

This is the work of God, that ye believe (John 6:29a). Belief, like faith, is a gift from God. Believing in God is not merely holding to the truth of His existence; it is the act of putting your faith in Him and in Him alone. Once this faith is secured, righteousness is imparted to us, and we are saved unto life eternal (James 2:23). **Believe on the Lord Jesus Christ, and thou shalt be saved** (Acts 16:31a).

Belief empowers us. It seals us with the Holy Spirit (Ephesians 1:13), justifies us by faith (Galatians 2:16), and emboldens us to speak of Christ (2 Corinthians 4:13). **For this cause also thank we God without ceasing, because, when ye received the word of God which ye heard of us, ye received it not as the word of men, but as it is in truth, the word of God, which effectually worketh also in you that believe** (1 Thessalonians 2:13).

Belief in Christ broadens our understanding and awakens us out of sleep (Romans 13:11). It assures us that we are the adopted children of God the Father, and that one day He will bring us into the inheritance of eternal glory.

Belief brings us into the body of Christ, giving us fellowship, like-mindedness, and togetherness (Acts 2:44). It establishes the unbreakable seal of salvation, in that those who are Christ's will never be lost (John 10:28). It elevates our citizenship, so that we are no longer of this world, but of the world that is to come.

Belief comes with an injunction. We are to be **careful to maintain good works** (Titus 3:8). By so doing, we **adorn the doctrine of God our Saviour in all things** (Titus 2:10b). When we show by our unwavering belief and faith in both God and His Word how confident we are, how unsullied, unafraid, and uncompromising, we are adorning the doctrine of God. We make it look good. We bring glory to God and blessings to all who know us.

When I first met my husband, his confidence and unabashed faith in Christ struck me. Up until that point in my life, I had known Christians as being weak and needy. When challenged, they crumbled. When questioned, they fell apart. Not so my man. He defended his faith and the Word of God like a champion and never backed down from the truth of the scriptures. He was bold in his belief in Christ and joyfully served God with integrity. He adorned the doctrine. So can you!

As women, we can be similarly uncompromising, but with the strength and power of gentleness and peaceable wisdom. I encourage you to base your belief on this verse: **Be still, and know that I am God** (Psalm 46:10a LXX). Whenever you waver, feel unsettled, attacked, or under stress, repeat that verse. Memorize the next verse, then the entire chapter, and turn your mind to the Words of Christ whenever stray thoughts beset you. Your faith will be bolstered, your hands will be empowered to live out God's will, and your mind will be renewed. Count on it.

How does belief in Christ fill up your soul? **He that believeth on me shall never thirst** (John 6:35b). Your belief in the doctrine of salvation, your assurance that God is real and that He is your heavenly Father, ready to avenge all injustice committed against you, will never leave you in want. He is the keeper of your soul, and He has filled you up with living water, which is the living Word. As long as you believe His Words to be true and follow them, knowing that they are Life, you will never go thirsty again.

After Gabriel gave Mary the astonishing news about her imminent pregnancy, she said, **Behold the handmaid of the Lord; be it unto me according to thy word** (Luke 1:38). What would you have said? Mary identified herself as the servant of the Lord and accepted His words. She chose to believe. And Elisabeth, when she heard the news, said, **blessed is she that believed: for there shall be a performance of those things which were told her from the Lord** (Luke 1:45).

2. **Fear me** (Jeremiah 32:39 LXX).

And fear not them which kill the body, but are not able to kill the soul: but rather fear him which is able to destroy both soul and body in hell (Matthew 10:28). My husband asked me to ponder a question today. The question was, "Why do you fear God?" I have a one-word answer: "hell".

No one wants to talk about hell. In fact, the word has been stricken even from the lips of preachers. However, how can we talk about heaven, love, humility, or courage, if we cannot talk about hell, hatred, pride, or fear? If we do not cultivate a healthy fear of the One who can send us to hell, what purpose do we ultimately have for our gratitude to Christ for receiving us into heaven?

Jesus humbled Himself, living the life of an earthling amidst the sully and despair of sinful humanity for one purpose, and one purpose only: to save us from hell. Without His sacrifice, you and I would be destined to live out our worst nightmares without the ability to ever wake up. Does that scare you? I fear Him who can deliver my soul to the depths of hell—and I love Him who is preserving my soul for the eternity of heaven.

Having a fear of the Lord does not in itself keep us from hell: **his salvation is *near* them that fear him** (Psalm 85:9b LXX, emphasis mine). We know that the demons fear him, but they are condemned (James 2:19). The fear of God precedes and inspires salvation. It is the *beginning* of wisdom, it motivates us to resist evil (Proverbs 3:7 LXX), it inspires obedience, and it directs us in the ways of the Lord. It blesses us. **How abundant is the multitude of thy goodness, O Lord, which thou hast laid up for them that fear thee!** (Psalm 31:19a LXX). The Lord is the strength of them that fear Him (Psalm 25:14a LXX), His eyes are on them that fear Him (Psalm33:18 LXX), and the word of salvation is sent to them that fear Him (Acts 13:26).

The most liberating and joy-inspiring fact about our fear of God is this—it gives us courage. King David writes: **the workers of iniquity . . . have not called upon God. There were they greatly afraid, where there was no fear** (Psalm 53:4b LXX). Where there is no fear of God, there is every reason to be afraid of the rudiments of the world. We fear God because we know that He is able to deliver or destroy the souls of us all. We know that He is an all-powerful, just, and holy God who will avenge all disobedience. By logically, emotionally, and fearfully placing our trust in Him, He becomes our Father, and here we are, on the playground of life, telling every bully around that our Dad is the toughest Dad in the universe. And so He is. **For ye have not received the spirit of bondage again to fear; but ye have received the Spirit of adoption, whereby we cry, Abba, Father** (Romans 8:15).

Fear not, little flock, for it is your Father's good pleasure to give you the kingdom (Luke 12:32). This verse prompts me to think of myself as a small child amidst many who stand in the presence of a great and wonderful King. The King may be a powerful giant who is fearsome to behold, but His eyes are tender towards me. I imagine that great and glorious King smiling down on me, encouraging me to do what is right so that He can bless me. He wants to bless you, too. You are His precious daughter, and there is nothing He wants more than to share His glorious kingdom with you.

Wise King Solomon said, **Hear the end of the matter, the sum: Fear God, and keep his commandments: for this is the whole man** (Ecclesiastes 12:13 LXX). Pious young Mary, who was also wise, said, **For**

he that is mighty hath done to me great things; and holy is his name. And his mercy is on them that fear him from generation to generation (Luke 1:49-50). If you follow these positive examples of what it means to be wise, you will be given mercy and fulfillment. Praise the Lord with fear, and rejoice in His mercy.

3. **Hearken unto me** (Leviticus 26:14 LXX).

Behold, I stand at the door and knock: if any man hear my voice, and open the door, I will come in to him; and will sup with him and he with me (Revelation 3:20). Those who hear the Lord to do His will are His. They are blessed and prospered for eternity.

Biblically speaking, for us to hear we need more than just ears because although we all have ears, we do not all hear. Jesus said to the Pharisees, **He that is of God heareth God's words: ye therefore hear them not, because ye are not of God** (John 8:47).

We, the saved in Christ, are Jesus' sheep. We rely on Him in faith and in trust, following Him about in order to ensure our safety, health, and prosperity. Jesus said, **my sheep hear my voice, and I know them, and they follow me** (John 10:27).

In Chapter Two, we learned what it meant to have "uncircumcised ears". Those whose ears are closed to the calling of the Lord do not belong to Him. The great mysteries of Biblical understanding, including the gospel of Christ, which is **the power of God unto salvation** (Romans 1:16a), is foolishness to them. Those who belong to Christ, however, **hear and understand** (Matthew 15:10b). They are blessed because they **hear the Word of God, and keep it** (Luke 11:28b). They will have eternal life, because **they that hear shall live** (John 5:25b).

Solomon entreats his son to hear him, to be wise, and to receive instruction. If he hears, Solomon says, **thou shalt receive for thine head a crown of graces, and a chain of gold around thy neck** (Proverbs 1:9 LXX). The son who hears his father's instruction will **be wise at thy latter end** (Proverbs 19:20b LXX). Solomon wrote, **Hear, my son, and receive my words; and the years of thy life shall be increased, that the resources of thy life may be many** (Proverbs 4:10 LXX).

When we hear God's voice, He will hear ours. **Now know that the Lord saveth his anointed; he will hear him from his holy heaven with the saving strength of his right hand** (Psalm 20:6 LXX). If we listen to the iniquity that is in our hearts instead of listening to God, He will not hear us. **If I have regarded iniquity in my heart, let not the Lord hearken to me. Therefore God has hearkened to me; he has attended to the voice of my prayer. Blessed be God, who has not turned away my prayer, nor his mercy from me** (Psalm 66:18-20 LXX).

How is our soul satisfied, prospered, and filled from hearing the Word of the Lord? Isaiah writes

> **Ye that thirst, go to the water, and all that have no money, go and buy; and eat and drink wine and fat without money or price. Wherefore do ye value at the price of money, and give your labour for that which will not satisfy? hearken to me, and ye shall eat that which is good, and your soul shall feast itself on good things. Give heed with your ears, and follow my ways: hearken to me, and your soul shall live in prosperity; and I will make with you an everlasting covenant, the sure mercies of David** (Isaiah 55:1-3 LXX).

No amount of money or information will give you what your soul yearns for. There is nothing on this earth that can satisfy your soul's longing for truth, righteousness, and justice. All that which you desire can only be fulfilled by God. His will is that your soul be fulfilled with His Word and His Way so that your glory will be requited with His in eternity. Feast on that which lasts forever: the words of our Lord Jesus Christ. Hearken unto Him and be blessed beyond belief. **Blessed is he that readeth, and they that hear the words of this prophecy, and keep those things which are written therein: for the time is at hand** (Revelation 1:3). Mary heard Gabriel's message. Although it sounded impossible, Mary chose to open her ears to the voice of the Lord in recognition of who He is and what He can do. He is God, in whom **all things are possible** (Matthew 19:26b). **He that spared not his own Son, but delivered him up for us all, how shall he not with him also freely give us all things?** (Romans 8:32). Like Mary, who was blessed among women, so can you be by your willingness to truly *hear* the words of God and *keep* them. His Words will fill up your soul to overflowing and your vessel will never run dry. Remember, God's words will never fall to the ground.[2]

4. **Learn of me** (Matthew 11:29).

For whatsoever things were written aforetime were written for our learning, that we through patience and comfort of the scriptures might have hope (Romans 15:4). In the Chapter One, I wrote that the Word is our textbook, the Holy Spirit is our teacher, and God is our examiner. The wisest among us recognize that they will always be students under godly trials. Until we humble ourselves enough to learn from God, proving that our hearts belong to Him, our ignorance will remain unresolvable, and the truth will forever elude us. **No one who will not learn righteousness on the earth, shall be able to do the truth** (Isaiah 26:10a LXX).

One of the most endearing and wonderful qualities about children is their desire and capacity to learn. But as a parent, what I find I can never teach enough of are lessons in righteousness. Doing that which is wrong comes easily. Doing that which is right takes hard work, self-discipline, repetition, and training. **And these words, all that I command thee this day, shall be in thy heart and in thy soul. And thou shalt teach them to thy children, and thou shalt speak of them sitting in the house, and walking by the way, and lying down, and rising up** (Deuteronomy 6:6-7 LXX). Just as children need instruction in righteousness repeated over and over again, so do we. **Thou hast commanded us diligently to keep thy precepts** (Psalm 119:4 LXX). How do we learn righteousness? By learning what pleases God. This means that we must learn His Word which is His truth and His will revealed to us through the fellowship of the Holy Spirit. Learning it is a lifelong labour which gives God glory. It is needful.

I therefore teach thee truth, and knowledge good to hear; that thou mayest answer words of truth to them that question thee (Proverbs 22:21 LXX). Those who walk in righteousness lead an exemplary life. They are noticed. Their company is sought by the wise, who seek to learn more from them. The more you seek to learn the "wisdom that is from above",

---

2   They will always come true, be substantiated, and fulfilled.

the more answers you will have, and the more exercised you will be in those things which are good. Paul tells us in Ephesians to **walk as children of light . . . Proving what is acceptable unto the Lord . . . . Wherefore be ye not unwise, but understanding what the will of the Lord is** (Ephesians 5:8b, 10, 17).

The wisdom that is from God above is bountiful, unchanging, and true. Those who know it humbly, gratefully, and joyfully receive it. They will be exalted (James 4:10). They will become wiser. **Thou hast made me wiser than mine enemies in thy commandment; for it is mine forever. I have more understanding than all my teachers; for thy testimonies are my meditation** (Psalm 119:98-99 LXX). They will have hope. **The eyes of your understanding being enlightened; that ye may know what is the hope of his calling, and what the riches of the glory of his inheritance in the saints** (Ephesians 1:18). They will inherit the earth. **Who is the man that fears the Lord? he shall instruct him in the way that he has chosen. His soul shall dwell in prosperity; and his seed shall inherit the earth** (Psalm 25:13 LXX).

One day while visiting Seattle, I was browsing in a Christian bookstore when I spotted an interesting quotation. I read and remembered it: "They themselves are makers of themselves by virtue of the thoughts which they choose and encourage".[3] When we choose to dwell on the Word of God, along with all those things which are "above" through prayer, recitation of scripture, and a chaste thought life, we are using the power of the Holy Spirit in order to obey God. This is our daily bread, that which is essential nourishment for life and growth in Christ. When unproductive or ungodly thoughts barge in, block them and replace them with the Word that you have memorized. This is precisely the manner by which we will become **wise unto that which is good, and simple concerning evil** (Romans 16:19b).

What a pleasure it is to humble ourselves by acknowledging that we are students, not masters. Love the Word. Dwell on it day and night. Commit yourself to learning it. Then stand by and observe the incredible rewards that it is God's good pleasure to give you. **Great peace have they that**

---

[3]   James Allen *As a Man Thinketh* (1902), available from http://jamesallen.wwwhubs.com/think.htm.

love thy law: and there is no stumblingblock to them (Psalm 119:165 LXX).

How does learning about Jesus prosper our souls? Jesus said, **Take my yoke upon you, and learn of me; for I am meek and lowly in heart: and ye shall find rest unto your souls** (Matthew 11:29). The confident knowledge as to the how and why we will spend eternity with our Saviour is the reward. Godliness and righteousness, holy and unblameable living are the rewards. Peace, self-discipline, and wisdom are the rewards. God's eternal love and protection of your soul are the rewards. **And if thou hadst hearkened to my commandments, then would thy peace have been like a river, and thy righteousness as a wave of the sea** (Isaiah 48:18 LXX). **Those things, which ye have both learned, and received, and heard, and seen in me, do: and the God of peace shall be with you** (Philippians 4:9).

Mary, the mother of Jesus, proved that she had "laboured in the word". She said

> **He hath shewed strength with his arm; he hath scattered the proud in the imagination of their hearts. He hath put down the mighty from their seats, and exalted them of low degree. He hath filled the hungry with good things; and the rich he hath sent empty away. He hath holpen his servant Israel, in remembrance of his mercy; As he spake to our fathers, to Abraham, and to his seed forever** (Luke 1:51-55).

By having learned the scriptures, Mary knew the works of God's hands. As a result, she knew exactly how and why to give Him praise.

5. **Love me** (John 14:23).

Thou shalt love the Lord thy God with all thy heart, and with all thy soul, and with all thy mind. This is the first and great commandment (Matthew 22:37-38). The basis of our regeneration in Christ is love. **God is love** (1 John 4:8b). It is the love of the Father, the grace of our Lord Jesus

Christ, and the communion of the Holy Spirit (2 Corinthians 13:14) that provide an everlasting citizenship with Christ for our souls.

There are three ways to illustrate our love for God. The first is to love His Word, the second is to obey His Word, and the third is to love one another.

King David wrote the longest chapter of the Bible based on his love for God's Word. **How I have loved thy law, O Lord! It is my meditation all the day** (Psalm 119:97 LXX). **I hate and abhor unrighteousness; but I love thy law** (Psalm 119:163 LXX). **Therefore have I loved thy commandments more than gold, or the topaz** (Psalm 119:127 LXX). David said that he loved God's Word so much that he deprived himself of sleep so that he could dwell on it. God was first in David's life. He sought God early in the morning and dwelled on the righteousness of God "all the day". So it is with all those who love the Lord sincerely.

Jesus said **If ye love me, keep my commandments** (John 14:15). Those who love God love to obey Him. Jesus said, **If a man love me, he will keep my words: and my Father will love him, and we will come unto him, and make our abode with him** (John 14:23). The love of God's Word translates into obedience, humility, and confidence. It supplies the believer with boldness before God: **Herein is our love made perfect, that we may have boldness in the day of judgment: because as he is, so are we in this world** (1 John 4:17). When we obey the Word, we are sanctified. Jesus said, **Now ye are clean through the word which I have spoken unto you** (John 15:3). Those who obey will have their hearts purged of sin. Isaiah wrote to the obedient: **And the Lord shall purge thy heart, and the heart of thy seed, to love the Lord thy God with all thy heart, and with all thy soul, that thou mayest live** (Isaiah 30:6 LXX).

The third way to illustrate our love for Christ is to love one another. **If we love one another, God dwelleth in us, and his love is perfected in us** (1 John 4:12b). My husband and I have a rule in our house that most people find strange. We do not, nor do we allow our children to use the word "love" for objects. We use it for people. You would be surprised at how limiting this simple rule can be. The word is used so flippantly in our society that people claim to love everything from their favourite toenail to a curly string of pasta! We believe that this habit, or oversight, has done irreparable harm to the Biblical concept of love. 1 Corinthians 13, the ever-quoted chapter on love would be ever so much richer if it were thoughtfully understood and applied.

Biblical love never wanes or grows weary because it is not based on our human capacity to love. It is based on the presence and strength of God's love that emanates from within us. It is completely self-sacrificial because it is a direct reflection of the love of Christ.

> **Hereby perceive we the love of God, because he laid down his life for us: and we ought to lay down our lives for the brethren. But whoso hath this world's good,**[4] **and seeth his brother have need, and shutteth up his bowels of compassion from him, how dwelleth the love of God in him?** (1 John 3:16-17).

If you tell someone you love them, then Biblically speaking, that means that you consider his or her life more valuable than your own and that you would die in that person's place given the chance. Do you love anyone like that? God loves you like that and proved it by sacrificing His Son. **Herein is love, not that we loved God, but that he loved us, and sent his Son to be the propitiation for our sins** (1 John 4:10). We are to love others in the same way that Christ loved us. Love can only prosper our souls if we give it away freely and joyfully.

Those whose love for God is as long as their laundry list have an unquenchable fire for God. Consider the life of Paul and the life of Mary Magdelene, both of whom were raised up out of the mire of sin and depravity to be placed in the loving embrace of the gospel truth. Contemplate the profoundness of Mary's love for Christ and be like her:[5] **Her sins, which are many, are forgiven; for she loved much: but to whom little is forgiven, the same loveth little** (Luke 7:47). Give your

---

[4]   That is, those who are able to provide for others because they have material wealth.

[5]   Please do not seek to live a sinful life and then repent of it later in order to share in the kind of love that Mary had. "God forbid". Hebrews 6 explains this, saying that to sin again after your conversion is to "crucify to themselves the Son of God afresh, and put him to an open shame" (Hebrews 6:6). Instead, renew your love for Christ by daily acknowledging the magnitude of His gift to you. Then share it with others.

love away with gratitude, rejoicing in the depth of the love that Christ gave away freely to you. It is so beautifully illustrated by Paul:

> **Who shall separate us from the love of Christ? shall tribulation, or distress, or persecution, or famine, or nakedness, or peril, or sword? As it is written, For thy sake we are killed all the day long; we are accounted as sheep for the slaughter. Nay, in all these things we are more than conquerors through him that loved us. For I am persuaded that neither death, nor life, nor angels, nor principalities, nor powers, nor things present, nor things to come, Neither height, nor depth, nor any other creature, shall be able to separate us from the love of God, which is in Christ Jesus our Lord** (Romans 8:35-39).

And we know that all things work together for good to them that love God, to them who are the called according to his purpose (Romans 8:28). Mary, who loved God even when she did not understand Him (Luke 2:50), was called according to His purpose. She fulfilled it, even though it meant that she had to endure the pain of a "pierced soul".

Jesus, born in the **fashion of a man** (Philippians 2:8a), was Mary's "natural" Son. Imagine her grief over His death as prophesied by Simeon:

> **And Simeon blessed them, and said unto Mary his mother, Behold, this child is set for the fall and rising again of many in Israel; and for a sign which shall be spoken against; (Yea, a sword shall pierce through thy own soul also,) that the thoughts of many hearts may be revealed** (Luke 2:34-35).

Love God enough to know that your ultimate good, despite what pain it may involve, is always ordained by the One who loves you. Only He is **able to do exceeding abundantly above all that we ask or think** (Ephesians 3:20a).

6. **Follow me** (John 10:27).

Jesus said **I am the way, the truth, and the life: no man cometh unto the Father, but by me** (John 14:6). In our culturally relative nation, we are daily pressured into compromising this essential truth in the name of relativism and tolerance. God wants us all to be saved (2 Peter 3:9). He is merciful (Psalm 100:5 LXX), longsuffering (Psalm 86:15 LXX), and full of pity (James 5:11). But He is not a liar (Titus 1:2). If He says that there is only one way to heaven and that way is through His Son, Jesus Christ our Lord, then those who attempt to enter into the kingdom by any other means will be rejected (John 10:1, 7, 9).

Neither is there salvation in any other: for there is none other name under heaven given among men, whereby we must be saved (Acts 4:12). That name is **Jesus Christ of Nazareth** (Acts 4:11b). He is God. Follow Him.

My husband shared it with me this way. The path to heaven which is the path of truth and righteousness that leads to eternal life is *straight*. It is the most direct path between two points. When we visit a place we have never been to, we take the straightest route to get there because it is the quickest and the least complicated. We do not veer to the right or to the left and risk getting lost. We stick to the simplest way. The way to God and our home in heaven is the same. It may be narrow and unworn, but it is straight, direct, and simple.

True Christians—followers of Christ—follow the straight path. They are radical in their willingness to lose the things of this world in order to **lay hold on eternal life** (1 Timothy 612a). They are like the disciples, who **forsook all, and followed [Jesus]** (Luke 5:11b).

What did the disciples forsake that we, too, should be willing to forsake? Jesus tells us:

> He that loveth father or mother more than me is not worthy of me: and he that loveth son or daughter more than me is not worthy of me. And he that taketh not his cross, and followeth after me, is not worthy of me. He that findeth his life shall lose it: and he that loseth his life for my sake shall find it (Matthew 10:37-39).

The follower of Christ does not try to find her Self; she loses her Self in order to find Christ. Similarly, she does not seek to preserve her life in this world; she seeks to lose it in order to gain eternal life in heaven.

When we are called to follow Christ, we are called to **follow after righteousness, godliness, faith, love, patience, meekness** (1 Timothy 6:11). **For even hereunto were ye called: because Christ also suffered for us, leaving us an example, that ye should follow his steps** (1 Peter 2:21). In the next verse, these steps are provided for us. They are the definitions for the virtues of godliness, faith, love, patience, and meekness quoted from 1st Timothy 6:11. If we are to **ever follow that which is good** (1 Thessalonians 5:15a), we are to do what He did.

What did Jesus do? **Who did no sin, neither was guile found in his mouth: Who, when he was reviled, reviled not again; when he suffered, he threatened not; but committed himself to him that judgeth righteously: Who his own self bare our sins** (1 Peter 2:22-24a). Phrase by phrase, here are these verses again, with the virtues extrapolated from the text. "Who did no sin, neither was guile found in his mouth": to be **godly** means to be without sin. "Who, when he was reviled, reviled not again": to be **meek** means to be mistreated without becoming defensive or retaliatory; "when he suffered, he threatened not": to be **patient** means to suffer for a long time with peace; "but committed himself to him that judgeth righteously": to have **faith** is to leave matters of judgment and justice to God. "Who his own self bare our sins in his own body": to **love** is to allow our Self to suffer, be deprived, or die for the sake of someone else.

Each of these situations is a reality for the follower of Christ within which her virtue can be exercised. She that follows the way of Jesus will find herself in situations that try, test, and prove her loyalty to the right way. As a result of her single-minded devotion to Christianity, the true follower of Christ is therefore hated by the world, just as He was.[6] **Marvel not, my brethren, if the world hate you** (1 John 3:13).

Rather than walk into the snares of death unawares, Christians have chosen to follow the Light, and be saved: **I am the light of the world: he**

---

[6]   John 15:19, "If ye were of the world, the world would love his own: but because you are not of the world, but I have chosen you out of the world, therefore the world hateth you."

that followeth me shall not walk in darkness, but shall have the light of life (John 8:12). Followers of Christ have the perfect guide. **Howbeit when he, the Spirit of truth, is come, he will guide you into all truth** (John 16:13a). By choosing to follow this perfect Guide, our path is lit (Psalm 119:105 LXX), our way is straight (Psalm 143:10 LXX), and the eyes of the Lord are ever upon us[7] (Psalm 32:8 LXX). By following Christ, we will never be without a Shepherd, a Counsellor, or a Father. **For this is our God for ever and ever: he will be our guide for evermore** (Psalm 48:14 LXX).

Christ is our Shepherd who leaves our souls in want of nothing (Psalm 23:1 LXX). In following Him there is hope, steadfastness, and safety.

> **From the ends of the earth have I cried to thee, when my heart was in trouble: thou liftedst me up on a rock thou didst guide me: because thou wert my hope, a tower of strength from the face of the enemy. I will dwell in thy tabernacle forever; I will shelter myself under the shadow of thy wings** (Psalm 61:2-4 LXX).

Those who follow Christ belong to God, as dear children. **For as many as are led by the Spirit of God, they are the sons of God** (Romans 8:14). They cannot be deceived: **And when he putteth forth his own sheep, he goeth before them, and the sheep follow him: for they know his voice. And a stranger will they not follow, but will flee from him: for they know not the voice of strangers** (John 10:4-5). Know the voice of God by following His Son, His Word.

> **For if wisdom shall come into thine understanding, and discernment shall seem pleasing to thy soul, good counsel shall guard thee, and holy understanding shall keep thee; to deliver thee from the evil way, and from the man that speaks nothing faithfully** (Proverbs 2:10-12 LXX).

Psalm 23 describes the state of the soul for those who are led and kept by God, the great Shepherd. David wrote, **He has restored my soul: he**

---

[7]   In other words, He will never turn His face away from us as He did when He "widowed" Jerusalem for their disloyalty.

has guided me into the paths of righteousness, for his name's sake (Psalm 23:3 LXX). Our Shepherd, who leads us in the right way, bringing our souls from the darkness of death to the brightness of life, receives glory when we follow Him.

Mary followed Him and she gave Him glory:

> **And Mary said, My soul doth magnify the Lord, And my spirit hath rejoiced in God my Saviour. For he hath regarded the low estate of his handmaiden: for, behold, from henceforth all generations shall call me blessed. For he that is mighty hath done to me great things; and holy is his name** (Luke 1:46-50).

STUDY BREAK
In Christ Jesus (Philemon 1:6)

Who are we in Christ? This is what the scriptures say, verbatim.

We are perfect, saved, sanctified, delivered, redeemed, washed, and reconciled. We are without condemnation, free from the law of sin and death, sons of God, new creatures. We are more than conquerors; we are victors.

We are crucified with Christ and raised with Christ. We are partakers of His promise and of His glory. We are of the same mind and of the same body. We are one.

In Christ, we are a chosen generation, a royal priesthood, a holy nation, a peculiar people. We are built upon the foundation of the apostles and prophets. We are healed. We are blessed. We have a high calling in God—a holy calling. We are created unto good works. We are loved.

We are children of light. We are purged from sin, renewed day by day, and complete. We are a sweet savour of Christ. We are the body of Christ, predestined, chosen, and precious. We are called to be saints, to be heirs of God and joint-heirs with Christ. We are ambassadors for Christ, fellow-workers and fellow-citizens with the saints. We are of the household of faith and of God. We are His.

In Him, we are sealed. We are in the Spirit. We are the temple of God. We are justified and we are holy. We are without sin.

7. **Abide in me** (John 15:4).

**I am the vine, ye are the branches: He that abideth in me, and I
in him, the same bringeth forth much fruit: for without me ye can
do nothing** (John 15:5). Jesus is our source of light and life. He is the
root without which we could never grow, receive sustenance, or bear fruit.
Without Him we are nothing and we can do nothing (John 15:5) because
those who are without Christ are dead in sin (Ephesians 2:1).

Not long ago, I was in a Christian bookstore that sold t-shirts. My
husband and I consider purchases made at Christian establishments as
opportunities to tithe. I found a few good t-shirts for my husband, but
was alarmed at what I found for women. Several of the shirts bore an
advertisement in laundry lists. In other words, they focused on imperfections
and flaws. It is a dreadful rallying cry to hear fellow sisters in Christ boast
over their faults and then erroneously call themselves good witnesses to
sinners for doing so. What could a sinner possibly hope to learn from
someone who is just as much a slave to sin as she is? Remember, children
of light are not slaves to sin; they are free unto life.

While it is true that when serving the flesh, we are imperfect and flawed,
it is also true that Christians have been cleansed from all unrighteousness (1
John 1:9) and are therefore unblameable (Colossians 1:22), unreproveable
(Colossians 1:22), sinless (1 John 3:6), and holy (1 Thessalonians 3:13).
This is not by virtue of our own merit, but by Jesus Christ's. That is an
advertisement in *His* righteousness, which is ours by blood. Now that is a
t-shirt I would wear!

It is for this reason that God places such importance on being good
examples (1 Timothy 4:12) and fruitful in good works (Colossians 1:10).
Our proof of being in Christ is not in our impulsion to sin, but in our
penchant for righteousness. Paul writes to the Colossians:

> **That ye might walk worthy of the Lord unto all pleasing,
> being fruitful in every good work, and increasing in the
> knowledge of God; Strengthened with all might, according
> to his glorious power, unto all patience with longsuffering
> and joyfulness; Giving thanks unto the Father, which hath
> made us meet to be partakers of the inheritance of the
> saints in light** (Colossians 1:10-12).

God's will is that we, as **little children, abide in him; that, when he shall appear, we may have confidence and not be ashamed before him at his coming** (1 John 2:28).

How do we stand firm in Christ in the guiltlessness and courage of sinless perfection? Jesus answers, **Abide in me, and I in you. As the branch cannot bear fruit of itself, except it abide in the vine; no more can ye, except ye abide in me** (John 15:4). The point of the entire matter rests on this single, inspiring verse: **Whosoever abideth in him sinneth not** (1 John 3:6a).

Every sin that you have ever committed or will ever commit has already been paid for. You are completely free from the burden of sin *if* you have taken on the righteousness of Christ through salvation. Jesus has **forgiven you all trespasses; Blotting out the handwriting of ordinances that was against us, which was contrary to us, and took it out of the way, nailing it to his cross** (Colossians 2:13b-14). In so doing, He triumphed over sin and death and hell and Satan for *you*. You are sealed forever in and by His righteousness—and you will never be lost (John 10:28). Your **life is hid with Christ in God** (Colossians 3:3b).

The Bishop of your soul (1 Peter 2:25) is the Keeper of your soul (1 Peter 4:19) and in Him is your hope fulfilled (Hebrews 6:11). The gift we have through Christ is more valuable than anything on this earth. This truth emboldens us in Christ with confidence, purpose, holiness, and power. It defines our ultimate worth and our priceless value as daughters of the living God. It is who we are. **Return to thy rest, O my soul; for the Lord has dealt bountifully with thee. For he has delivered my soul from death, mine eyes from tears, and my feet from falling** (Psalm 116:7-8 LXX).

While those around her marvelled that the baby in the manger was called Christ the Lord, **Mary kept all these things, and pondered them in her heart** (Luke 2:19). Moses told the Israelites: **Consider in thine heart, that the Lord thy God he is God** (Deuteronomy 4:39 LXXa). When young Jesus claimed to be about His Father's business in the temple, Mary did not understand what He meant, but she **kept all these sayings in her heart** (Luke 2:50-51b). King David kept all of God's words in his heart (Psalm 119:11 LXX). Those who meditate on God's words are blessed (Psalm 1:2 LXX). Mary was blessed. David was blessed. Will you be blessed? **If ye abide in me, and my words abide in you, ye shall ask what ye will, and it shall be done unto you** (John 15:7).

Modern Snapshot
KATHRYN

Kathryn is the youngest of five. She was rather spoiled growing up, receiving from her aged parents privileges that her older siblings had not. Like all children who sin without punishment, by the time Kathryn reached the age of accountability, she was carrying in her heart the guilt of a tortured and sinful soul. It led her to take on habits of self-loathing. Suicidal, lazy, and overweight, Kathryn was on a path that led to eternal—if not physical—death.

One day a Christian man came into her family's life. He did not go to church. He did not lead a Bible Study, nor did he have a seminary degree. He was a simple, blue-collar worker who had a heart for God. Having such a heart made him wise in the ways of the Lord. He knew right from wrong, truth from falsehood, and lost from found. Immediately he understood that the need of Kathryn's heart was for the reconciliation that can only come through Christ.

Although her opportunities to learn from this man were limited, Kathryn quickly recognized her need for Christ. Embracing the reality of the Bible, she immersed herself in the Word day and night. Unfettered by older siblings who tried to dissuade her from the right path, she persisted in the way of Christ. She chose to lay down her sins at the feet of the cross and accept God's gift of eternal life.

Today she ministers to an unsaved husband, manages a hobby farm, and meditates on the gospel of Christ. She is able to discern truth from falsehood because she knows the voice of her Shepherd. She is able to edify and encourage her sisters in Christ because she has in her the hope of eternal life through Jesus Christ our Lord. She is a precious and holy daughter of the King of kings and Lord of lords, who is both powerful and mighty to tear down the knowledge that is not of Christ in order to build us up in the Truth.

Kathryn is no longer either lazy or depressed. Although she is still young, she is wise. It is her desire to do the will of God, to win souls to Christ, and to bear the fruits of righteousness and peace. It is not age that makes us wise, it is the indwelling of the Word and the Spirit of God coupled with our determination to deny our own will in order to do the will of God. So it is with all those who name the name of the Lord Jesus Christ as their Saviour, their Eternal King. Kathryn's reward, which is in heaven, will be great. What will your reward be?

For he that is mighty hath done to me great things; and holy is his name (Luke 1:49).

Summary

Those who have suffered as true children of the living God have sacrificed their Self to become obedient even unto death. They are radical in their desire to be faithful servants of the living God. They believe Him, fear Him, and hearken to Him. They learn from Him, love Him, and follow Him. In Him, they will abide forever. Their soul will find its rest in Him as its great and eternal reward. They daily purge their sin by walking in the Spirit of the Lord. Their souls are prospered and blessed. Is yours?

If you love the Lord for what He did for you, thank Him by living a life worthy of the inheritance of a holy princess. Read His Word, and do what it says!

Who Shall Deliver Me?

- **Keep my soul, and deliver me: let me not be ashamed; for I have hoped in thee** (Psalm 25:20 LXX).
- **Pity me, O Lord; for I am weak: heal me, O Lord; for my bones are vexed. My soul also is grievously vexed: but thou, O Lord, how long? Return, O Lord, deliver my soul: save me for thy mercy's sake** (Psalm 6:2-4 LXX).
- **For thou hast chosen my soul, that it should not perish: and thou hast cast all my sins behind me** (Isaiah 38:17 LXX).

How Can I Purge My Sin?

1. Put on the helmet of salvation (Ephesians 6:17).
2. Receive the gift of the Spirit (1 Timothy 4:14).
3. Be washed in the blood of the Lamb (Revelation 7:14).
4. Learn the Word (John 15:3).
5. Cultivate godly repentance (2 Corinthians 7:10).
6. Be reconciled to God (2 Corinthians 5:20).
7. Be partakers of the Lord's suffering (1 Peter 4:13).

Think on These Things

1. How can I have good thoughts?
   Phil. 2:5, 13, Col. 3:2, Rom. 12:2

2. How can I thank God without ceasing?
   1 Thess. 2:13

3. How do I experience God's strength?
   2 Cor. 12:10

4. How can I develop self-control?
   Psalm 55:22, Rom. 8:2, 2 Cor. 10:4,5

5. How do I keep strong?
   Jude 21, 24 John 15:4, Col. 3:16, 17

6. How do I hear God?
   Ps. 44:1, Ps. 46:10

7. Is there a time God does not hear us?
   Ps. 66:18-20

8. Does real satisfaction exist here on earth?
   Is. 55:1-3

9. How can I cope with rejection?
   1 John 3:13, 16 Rom. 8:35-39

10. Is there really only one way to heaven?
    John 14:6

11. How can I learn righteousness?

Ps. 119:144, Is. 48:18, Phil. 4:9

12. Should I ever be afraid of God?

Ps. 27:1, 1 Jn. 4:10, Lk. 1:49-50

13. How can I calm my soul?

Ps. 131, Col. 3:2

14. What does God require from us?

Mic. 6:8

15. How can I praise God?

Ps. 100

Epilogue

**And I will bring the blind by a way that they knew not,
and I will cause them to tread paths which they have
not known: I will turn darkness into light for them, and
crooked things into straight. These things will I do,
and will not forsake them.**
(Isaiah 42:16 LXX)

Godly Sorrow

If in reading this book, you have been made to see errors in your way, rejoice! This is an indication that you are indeed a daughter of the living God. You have proven your love for Him by desiring to do His will. This humility will endear you to Christ, motivating Him to answer your prayers and help you do what your flesh is powerless to accomplish on its own. **And he said unto me, My grace is sufficient for thee: for my strength is made perfect in weakness. Most gladly therefore will I rather glory in my infirmities, that the power of Christ may rest upon me** (2 Corinthians 12:9).

In 2 Corinthians 7, Paul spoke the truth with boldness to the Corinthians. He said, **For though I made you sorry with a letter, I do not repent, though I did repent: for I perceive that the same epistle hath made you sorry, though it were but for a season** (2 Corinthians 7:8). The truth, spoken boldly, has the power to injure. The injury is painful, uncomfortable, and discouraging, but temporary. Without an injury, there can be neither hope nor healing. **And our hope of you is stedfast, knowing, that as ye are partakers of the sufferings, so shall ye be also of the consolation** (2 Corinthians 1:7).

Now I rejoice, not that ye were made sorry, but that ye sorrowed to repentance: for ye were made sorry after a godly manner, that ye might receive damage by us in nothing (2 Corinthians 7:9). Paul's rejoicing came when he realized that the Corinthians allowed themselves to feel the pain of their sin and repent of it. It is far more damaging to withhold the truth or leave it unheeded than it is to hear it, suffer it, and allow the conviction to change our hearts for God's glory. **Therefore I take pleasure in infirmities, in reproaches, in necessities, in persecutions, in distresses for Christ's sake: for when I am weak, then am I strong** (2 Corinthians 12:10).

A withheld or unheeded truth is like a leprous hand which is numb to pain. A wound is received, but is not felt, so it is left untreated. It festers and grows worse and worse, until eventually the entire hand is lost. If a brother or sister in Christ does not love us enough to bring us to feel the pain of our sin, we could be walking around with it and not even know it. Trustworthy are **the wounds of a friend** (Proverbs 27:6 LXX) who loves you in Christ enough to tell you the truth with wisdom and patience.

To whom are you a loving friend? Are you ready to gently admonish your sisters in Christ, living your life as a godly example for them to follow? Are you able to remember Bible verses that can open a friend's heart or lead a soul to Christ? Live your life for God. Learn to be a real Titus 2 woman and minister to the young women around you. They need you to be right now what they should be in the future.

Worldly Sorrow

For godly sorrow worketh repentance to salvation not to be repented of: but the sorrow of the world worketh death (2 Corinthians 7:10). When we feel worldly sorrow, we are feeling the self-pity of an offended ego, which is our selfish response to not getting our own way. While it is common to initially respond with resistance to the truth, this reaction is often temporary, while our spirit wrestles with our flesh to bring our hearts under obedience to Christ. Conversely, there are those who receive admonition and persist in responding with defiance or self-justification. Such people probably do not belong to the Lord. They may think that they do, but they have deceived themselves in their hearts. By refusing to receive the chastening of God the Father, they are proving that they are not His children. They belong to the world and their ego is their god.

Could this describe you? Did you respond in anger to the admonition in this book? Did you mock, dismiss, or disdain the messages herein, me, the messenger, or God, the examiner of your heart? If so, I want you to know that I would love to meet you and give you a big hug. You may not know it yet, but you really need one! You are loved, and no amount of hatred or hostility on your part will change the desire I have in my heart to see that you come to know the love of Christ.

Where do you stand right now with Jesus Christ? Have you disobeyed the Word of God? Let's see. Have you lied to a friend, dishonoured a parent, wanted something that was not yours, or used the Lord's name carelessly? Have you hated your sister, your spouse, your parent, or your neighbour? The poignancy of the law is that it convicts us all. Not one of us can stand before a holy and just God and claim to be good. **There is none good but one, that is, God** (Matthew 19:17).

No matter how good we try to be, none of us can maintain the high standard of God's law. **I had not known sin, but by the law** (Romans 7:7). The punishment for our sin—no matter how great or small it is—is death. **For the wages of sin is death** (Romans 6:23a). This knowledge places on our hearts a tremendous burden of sin. Do you know what God did for you to alleviate this burden that we all share? **For God so loved the world, that he gave his only begotten Son, that whosoever believeth in him should not perish but have everlasting life** (John 3:16).

Jesus, who was God in the flesh, died on the cross so that His shed blood would pay, in full, the debt for your sin. You and I both deserved that death because we sinned against God. But because of His immeasurable love for us, Jesus took our sins to Himself to rescue us from the clutches of the devil and from the flames of hell. He is our Saviour, **the Lamb of God, which taketh away the sin of the world** (John 1:29).

We may choose to omit our sins from conscious thought, refusing to acknowledge them, but ignoring them does not make them go away. That would be like refusing to acknowledge gravity; it will affect us even if we ignore or deny it. Those who do not read the Bible to know the law nevertheless **shew the work of the law written in their hearts, their conscience also bearing witness** (Romans 2:15b). What is in your heart?

The unregenerate heart becomes scarred from the effects of sin when denial renders us unrepentant. Unconfessed sin eats at our souls like a cancer, causing anger, turmoil, insecurity, and guilt. God has offered us freedom from these plaguing self-recriminations. It is through the confession of sin, the forgiveness of sin, and the turning away from sin (repentance). **If we confess our sins, he is faithful and just to forgive us our sins, and to cleanse us from all unrighteousness** (1 John 1:9). Kneel before Him and pray, asking Him to forgive you. Believe that you are forgiven. Then, stand firm and **hold fast the confidence and the rejoicing of the hope firm unto the end** (Hebrews 3:6). Finally, **go, and sin no more** (John 8:11b).

If this book has changed your heart or your life, please write me and let me know. If you are struggling and in need of help, please look to the Word of God first and then let me know how I can help. My family and I would be privileged to add you to our prayer list. Write us at swifttohear@ mail.com.

> **Now unto him that is able to keep you from falling,**
> **and to present you faultless before the presence of his**
> **glory with exceeding joy,**
> **To the only wise God our Saviour, be glory and majesty,**
> **dominion and power, both now and ever. Amen.**
> (Jude 1:24-25)

INDEX

doctrine xv, 15, 38, 40, 41, 47, 51,
52, 74, 91, 104, 118, 131,
132, 139, 150, 151

E

equipped 75
EVE 110
evil 8, 9, 10, 11, 13, 14, 16, 17, 18,
19, 22, 23, 24, 26, 29, 39,
45, 46, 47, 48, 49, 50, 51,
52, 54, 57, 69, 73, 81, 92,
97, 100, 102, 103, 107, 108,
110, 111, 117, 118, 119, 123,
134, 138, 139, 152, 156, 163
eyes ix, 5, 11, 26, 33, 40, 47, 50,
54, 70, 73, 76, 86, 89, 97,
100, 111, 117, 122, 146, 152,
156, 163, 166

F

fear 5, 25, 36, 41, 53, 54, 58, 98,
115, 118, 128, 146, 148, 151,
152, 153
Fear me 149, 151
fellowship 70, 81, 135, 150, 155
Fickle 74
Flattery 68, 69, 70
Follow me 149, 161
foolish 9, 10, 11, 14, 16, 17, 18, 19,
21, 22, 25, 58, 91, 128
Fruitful
labour 107
fruits of righteousness 18, 42, 97, 168
Full Soul
blesssed 147

G

glory vii, ix, x, xii, xv, xvi, 2, 10, 18,
26, 27, 29, 30, 32, 42, 46,
47, 50, 53, 55, 57, 58, 66,
82, 92, 93, 97, 99, 106, 107,
108, 110, 113, 114, 122, 123,
124, 130, 131, 132, 133, 136,
137, 138, 150, 154, 155, 156,
164, 171, 172
glory of the man
image of God 110, 130
Godly Sorrow 171
God's blessings 34
good conversation 56, 76, 137
good works xv, 5, 32, 79, 91, 107,
136, 150, 164, 165
great price 32, 33, 79
guile 51, 162
Gwen 56, 57
GWEN 56

H

Hard of Heart 25
harlot 60, 65, 68, 70, 71, 78, 82,
100
hear 31, 34, 37, 38, 39, 41, 45, 53,
67, 69, 81, 103, 104, 108,
113, 146, 147, 153, 154, 155,
165, 169, 172
Hearken to me 149
heart vii, xi, xii, xvi, xvii, 1, 2, 6, 9,
10, 11, 13, 14, 16, 18, 20,
22, 25, 26, 27, 29, 32, 33,
34, 35, 36, 37, 39, 41, 42,
43, 48, 50, 51, 53, 57, 66,
67, 68, 69, 70, 71, 72, 73,
75, 76, 77, 79, 81, 82, 88,
95, 96, 114, 115, 128, 133,
134, 135, 137, 138, 139, 141,
143, 146, 148, 154, 155, 157,
158, 163, 167
holy ix, 4, 16, 47, 58, 82, 83, 98,
102, 106, 107, 112, 121, 122,
127, 129, 134, 148, 152, 153,
154, 157, 163, 164, 165, 167,
168, 173
Hophni and Phinehas 16
How Does a Woman Display Foolishness? 9
humility vii, 1, 14, 22, 43, 54, 85,
120, 141, 151, 158, 171
husband vii, x, xii, 8, 9, 10, 13, 21,